THE CRAFT OF STICKMAKING

The Craft of
STICKMAKING

Leo Gowan

The Crowood Press

First published in 1991 by
The Crowood Press Ltd
Ramsbury, Marlborough
Wiltshire SN8 2HR

Paperback edition 2000
This impression 2001

British Library Cataloguing-in-Publication Data

A catalogue record for this book is available from the British Library.

ISBN 1 86126 375 9

Acknowledgements
Photographs by Bob Graham
Line-drawings by Frank Day
Miniature sticks and The Show by Sheila Attree

My thanks are due to many stickmaking friends for their advice and
encouragement and also for offering their sticks for illustrations. It is
impossible to name them all but I must express my debt particularly to
Sheila and Fred Attree, Bill Canning, Frank Day, Brian Hampshire, Dave
Owens, Brian Thomas and Alan Thompson.

Typeset by Keyboard Services, Luton, Beds.
Printed and bound in Great Britain by
Bookcraft (Bath) Ltd.
Midsomer Norton, Somerset.

Contents

	Introduction	7
1	Shanks	8
2	Tools and Equipment	15
3	One-Piece Sticks	21
4	Block Sticks	25
5	Wood Handles	29
6	Burrs	33
7	Deer Antler	36
8	Deer Foot Handles	46
9	Horn	48
10	Plain Horn Handles	54
11	Fancy Horn Handles	66
12	Horn Disc Sticks	73
13	Assembling the Stick	75
14	Finishing	80
15	Miniature Sticks	82
16	Shows and Judging	87
	Appendix	91
	Index	95

This book is dedicated to Leonard Parkin,
horncraftsman and master stickmaker

Introduction

It is heartening to find that stickmaking, which is part of an enduring rural culture centuries old, is enjoying greater popularity than ever. It is an absorbing subject and one which has no limit. Using natural materials and skills which can be acquired fairly easily, articles which are functional, have character, and are attractive, can be made. Many sticks become old and trusted friends, appreciated for their qualities in day-to-day use, companionable and versatile. Others will have the innate attraction of folk art, with the carved or shaped heads of perhaps animals, birds or fish. And the tools needed are minimal; many show-winning sticks have been fashioned with a pocket-knife.

However, the literature on the craft is scant, and not very forthcoming with regard to actual methods. This book should redress the balance, being a combination of ideas, trials (and errors), folklore, and the knowledge I have gained from others during a period of forty years.

1 Shanks

WHERE TO OBTAIN SHANKS

Shanks are often seen for sale nowadays. Country fair stalls commonly have them, and fishing tackle and gun shops can usually oblige. They have the advantage that they are already seasoned, varnished, and also fitted usually with a metal tip or ferrule. The length is generally 4–4½ft (1.2–1.4m) which is adequate for most purposes, and they come already straightened. As far as I know, they are only available in hazel or blackthorn. The drawback is the cost; especially when – even if you only intend to make up one stick – it is advisable to have several shanks from which to make your choice. It is also far more satisfying to cut and season your own. Fortunately I have always lived in well-wooded areas of the countryside and have never needed to buy a shank myself.

When living in the Lake District, I always found that permission to cut was readily given by the National Trust and, as they were the biggest landowners in large areas of the National Park, I had no trouble obtaining as many shanks as I required. The Forestry Commission, too, will normally oblige (the person to approach in each instance is the Head Forester). Hazel, blackthorn and holly are normally cut back in woods when planting-out is undertaken, and brashed regularly thereafter as scrub wood, and left to rot or end up on the bonfire. Disused railway embankments are often the source of some really good shanks, particularly thorn, and similarly roadside banks. Hedgerows can be good, particularly if overgrown or, better still, cut and laid a few years previously, and most farmers will allow you to cut with discretion. Odd shanks can sometimes be had in local parks or even private gardens. And once you get an eye for a stick you will find that you begin to see them all over – along roadsides when driving, by river banks and streams, old quarries, even in churchyards. Permission to cut is usually readily given, and an offer of a stick will rarely be refused!

COMMONEST WOODS

Hazel

Hazel is by far the most popular shank and deservedly so. It is common in most parts of the country and usually easily available, being a non-commercial timber, apart from in odd areas where it is coppiced for hurdle and basket making. The shoots normally grow from the base and are often obligingly straight and if not can be easily straightened. The taper along the length is not usually too pronounced, and its strength and resilience make it a universal favourite with stickmakers. Of all sticks it has by far the greatest range of colour variations in the bark, from dark brown, through paler shades often with a constrasting mottle, to a very light type, called 'white' or 'silver' hazel in the North and Scotland, where it is commonest. There is also, in Scotland, an extremely eye-catching variation of the latter which has the light bark tinged with a pinkish cast. This only grows where there is a thin soil covering over basaltic rock. Occasionally one can come across another light-coloured bark variation, but this is caused by mosaic disease which has the effect of bleaching the brown of the bark and leaving it with contrasting black veins. These sticks are always greatly prized but when found must be cut as soon as practicable as the disease kills the bush eventually.

Ash

Ash makes a good sturdy, practical country stick but its homely, rather coarse, grey-green bark is not to everyone's taste. However, if you buff it down with steel wool (Grade 3 – coarse) and are careful not to rub too vigorously, you will be left with a pleasing green underbark with brownish and grey mottles, flecks and streaks. For some reason, ash always seems to thrive along old railway cuttings or by the side of the track. It does not grow as straight as hazel but can be straightened easily enough, and tends to taper rather quickly at times. The best-balanced sticks

can usually be had where there is a woodland canopy making the sticks draw up towards the light. Coniferous woods are particularly good in this respect but you must get there before the growth is too thick which kills off all underplanting.

Holly

The moisture content of holly is very high, making it a difficult timber to season. The fine, close grain makes it relatively heavy, and it is usually well branched. You will rarely be able to make a holly stick with the bark left on as it invariably wrinkles and loosens as it seasons due to the excess moisture. Immediately after cutting a holly shank, seal the cut ends before storing to prevent splitting. I find knotting or knot sealer the most efficient – preferably two coats. Cut the branches off leaving perhaps 1in (5cm) stumps. Do not cut off flush with the shank. Seal the cut ends of these branches too, otherwise they will each form a split or check which runs back into the main shank. When seasoned, some of the bark will be loose and can be pulled off but a method will need to be devised to remove the remainder. I leave the shanks out on the lawn for a few nights and when well dampened, the bark is easily scraped off with an old knife or something similar. You will find that the bark has stained the shank an olive shade but if you buff this down with emery cloth the timber will be very light coloured, quite often with the grain pattern producing a beautiful watermark effect after staining.

In the North, a practice has evolved of cutting holly shanks up to 3–5in (7.5–13cm) in diameter. After the required seasoning, of anything up to five years, they are then rasped and trimmed down to normal dimensions, and the watermark figuration is often quite pronounced. There are several disadvantages with this system: cut, say, three of these monsters and you have quite a weight to carry – equal to about twenty or so hazel shanks of the same length. Then you have the long seasoning period, and finally the laborious task of reducing to normal dimensions – and all for a watermark which is quite often present in a normal-size shank in the first instance! However, a well-finished holly shank with a prominent watermark and knots left proud, makes a very desirable stick indeed and repays amply the time expended on it.

Blackthorn

Blackthorn is regarded by many as the ultimate shank for a stick. It is a very hard, close-grained wood and if growing from the trunk of the tree or bush, is covered with very sharp, vicious spines. It spreads through root suckers, which can throw up long, straight and, unfortunately, usually spineless shoots. The two principal attractions of the blackthorn are the deep red bark and the knots, which are best when left proud. A simple blackthorn-knob stick is the prized possession of many an aged countryman; offer any stickmaker a choice of shanks and the most popular choice would always be this wood. You need old clothes and a tightly fitting cap if you are going to get amongst the blackthorn, as you will rarely find a decent stick growing on the outside of the bush. The best ones I have found were on the fringe of a conifer plantation where the blackthorn had been cut down to ground level when the wood was planted some five years earlier. Some lovely shanks had sprouted from the old stumps. Occasionally a good find can be made in an old hedgerow, especially if laid

previously, resulting in new vertical growth. Big old bushes which have spread by suckers into quite extensive thickets are not usually so good, as they, like all thorns left to themselves, get into a real tangle with few straight growths.

It is essential also when cutting black-thorn to wear thorn-proof gloves. If, by chance, a thorn is lodged under your skin, try to remove it as soon as is practicable as the bark contains a powerful irritant and festering will occur very quickly. A pair of secateurs will be needed as it is impossible to carry blackthorn without removing the thorns. Being close-grained it is a heavy wood, and you will have difficulty carrying more than ten decent shanks (if you should be so lucky!) at one go. Leave little stumps on the thorns as, like holly, it is prone to checking in to the shank. Being a heavy timber you will never see a shepherd with a working crook of blackthorn because it lacks ease of handling, but for a practical, sturdy yet showy stick for country use this can not be bettered. It is essential to seal cut ends before storing as otherwise it will split.

OTHER WOODS

Hawthorn

Hawthorn can be obtained occasionally from hedgerows but is prone to taper quickly. It is not very often that a good, well-balanced 4ft (1.2m) shank can be obtained but 3ft ones (90cm) are common enough. It is a rather similar wood to black-thorn, liable to be a little heavy as it has a tight grain. Leave the knots standing proud and if the nondescript, rather coarse, greyish bark is buffed down with steel wool, a pleasant shade of reddish-brown is revealed in the underbark. A good hawthorn shank makes an acceptable substitute for blackthorn and indeed has often been passed off as such.

Fruitwoods

These include apple, cherry, crab, damson, pear and plum. They are all strong and tough with a fine, even grain and can occasionally be found in suitable lengths. Most have uninteresting bark but occasionally a plum or damson can be obtained with a deep red colour, reminiscent of blackthorn. They will often have numerous side shoots and if de-barked, the resulting knots can add an attractive feature to what is otherwise an unremarkable shank.

Mountain Ash or Rowan

This is very common in Scotland and the North. It is inclined to be twiggy but trimmed, these make nice knots. The bark is rather uninteresting being a plain grey shade but as it is smooth it polishes well. It is prone to taper too quickly for suitably sized shanks to be easily available even where common, but a good, well-balanced one can hold its own with most.

Conifers

Conifers are usually held to be useless for stickmaking but I have seen extremely attractive shanks made from spruce. The bark had been left on whilst seasoning and then peeled, leaving the shank stained in a most unusual reddish-brown shade. They were very lightweight but exceptionally tough and durable as the fibres in the timber are very long and well-knitted together. This would not be everybody's choice but is worth consideration if only for the novelty. Conifers also include yew from which a shank can sometimes be found. The bark is very rough and needs to be removed after seasoning. The wood is red-brown in colour and reasonably attractive, quite often with a nice grain.

DIMENSIONS

A good length to cut shanks is 4–4½ft (1.2–1.4m), though any lengths between 3–6ft (0.9–1.8m) should not be ignored; all are useful at some time. The most popular diameter is around the 1in (2.5cm) mark – varying from 1⅛in (2.9cm) down to ¾in (1.9cm) – and with a gradual taper, or occasionally none at all. A good, well balanced shank would taper over a 4ft (1.2m) length from approximately 1in (2.5cm) down to not less than ⅝in (1.5cm). Any stick that tapers to half its diameter over its length is badly balanced. Do not discard sticks with an oval cross-section (a common feature of holly and blackthorn) as antler, in particular, will often have the same shape and so a good match-up between handle and shank can be obtained without trimming.

SEASONING

In the timber trade the norm for seasoning is 1in (2.5cm) (thickness) per year. A standard 1in thick shank will normally be ready for stickmaking within a year, but taking the bark into consideration the wood will be less than 1in and so the shank can be used earlier. I have often made up sticks in August and September from shanks cut the previous November. However, holly and blackthorn, being

11

very close-grained, will usually need a full year. Tie all shanks as tightly as possible in bundles and store under cover. I have always used a garage or shed for storing but a porch or even an empty store-room would do. Keep them away from central heating. Prop up the bundles against a wall but never be tempted to stretch them across rafters as they will tend to sag and you will have a lot of straightening to do. Fortunately, I have never had trouble with woodworm in my shanks but attacks can be prevented by standing the bundles in a bucket of *clear* wood preservative for a day or two, then reversing the bundles in the solution before storing. A strong-smelling, creosoted garden shed usually acts as a good deterrent also.

DEBARKING

Holly is the commonest wood to be de-barked but never do this until seasoned as the shank will be ruined by longitudinal splits. Try to leave the knots standing proud as they are much admired by most enthusiasts. The wood must then be stained as it is pale and featureless in its natural state. Ash can also be debarked successfully, resulting in a nice honey-coloured timber with a distinctive grain pattern. Although it is a crime to debark blackthorn with its lovely bark, sometimes this is the only way to utilize an otherwise too heavy or unwieldy shank. Norman Tulip, the famous Northumberland stick dresser, whose collection of fancy, carved horn-headed sticks is renowned, has always favoured stripped holly shanks. He feels that this kind of shank better com-plements the intricately carved heads than hazel or blackthorn and, having seen his collection, I am inclined to agree.

STAINING

I have never used commercial stains. On a stripped shank a first class stain can be made with a spoonful of instant coffee dis-solved in ¼in (0.6cm) of boiling water in a cup. This looks very dark but when applied with a piece of clean rag shows as light olive. It can be darkened, if required, by further applications. To really empha-size the figuring in the grain of a holly, try experimenting with a wash of indian ink. You will be horror-struck when you first apply it as it has a matt black finish, but wipe over immediately with a damp cloth and the grain pattern will emerge. It is advisable to experiment with this type of staining using a length of off-cut stick before actually trying it out on a valued shank.

For a darker shade of stain, dissolve some potassium permanganate crystals in hot water. Experiment with the strength until you reach a desired depth of colour, bearing in mind that deeper shades also result from repeated applications. When initially applied this stain is a deep purple shade but changes in seconds to a rich dark reddish-brown. It is perfect for disguising any imperfections in the bark of a dark hazel or blackthorn, or in jointing when the bark has been buffed down in places and the bare wood is exposed. If a slightly redder shade is wanted, add red ink.

STRAIGHTENING

Few shanks are perfectly straight when cut. Do not be put off by even pronounced bends as they can be removed easily after seasoning. You will be wasting your time in trying to straighten them before then as they will gradually creep back to their for-

A straightening board.

mer shape. Try to avoid a dog-leg unless you are desperate because even if straightened successfully, there will normally be an enlarged knuckle where the main bend was originally.

Consult with other stickmakers or study the literature on the subject and you will be offered a plethora of conflicting advice on how to straighten sticks: stretch them over your knee (just try doing that with a holly or blackthorn), in a vice, in a notched

wood 'horse', with a jack, by suspending weights from them; or heat with a fan heater, a hot-air gun, a naked flame, a steaming kettle; cover with foil, sacking, a damp cloth – your mind reels with the possibilities.

I have straightened many hundreds of sticks easily and quickly with a hot-air gun or a hair dryer on the highest setting. Make a straightening board from hardwood (mine is oak) 6in (15cm) long by 3–4in (7.5–

10cm) wide, and preferably at least 1¼in (3.2cm) thick (1½in (3.9cm) is ideal). In this board drill three holes of 2in (5cm), 1½in (3.9cm) and 1in (2.5cm) in diameter. Obtain two or three shortish lengths of thick rubber hose, such as car radiator hose, which will fit in these holes. Heat the bent part of the shank along a 4–5in (10–13cm) length – this allows the fibres to stretch – then place the heated part in the appropriate hole according to size, bear down slightly against the bend and it will straighten easily. Hazel and ash may require two or three minutes heating only but give holly and blackthorn five minutes. The rubber collar will prevent bruising or denting. When heating, play the hot air back and forth along the area to be treated and turn the shank round continuously to prevent scorching. Remove the stick from the board and, when satisfied as to straightness, wet the heated area with a fine spray of cold water. An indoor plant mist spray is ideal but if not, cool down for a few seconds under running water. If the heated part is not cooled quickly in this way there is a slight tendency for the stick to revert to its bent state.

WHEN TO CUT

Cut your shanks when the sap is down, in November, December and January. If cut at other times, they will require a longer time to season and, more importantly, could very likely suffer from bark wrinkling and, worse still, cracking or checking in the cut ends. If not too pronounced, wrinkled bark can be made into an attractive feature by buffing down lightly with fine-grade steel wool which hopefully will result in a snakeskin effect. Checking can be avoided by sealing the cut ends with knotting (use two coats).

TOOLS

A knife, however sharp, is not much good for cutting shanks, as you will never be able to make a clean through-cut, rather you will have to nibble away all round. In a thick bush this can often be very nearly impossible. I have found that the best tool for stick cutting is a Bridgedale Japanese folding pruning saw. This has a blade with extremely sharp teeth which are hard-chrome plated, stain resistant and virtually rust free. The blade cuts, like all Japanese saws, on the pull stroke, and I find that it can easily cut through a 1-inch hazel shank with one stroke. It has a very useful blade-locking device which prevents the blade closing accidentally on the fingers, and also a bright orange plastic handle which can easily be seen if the saw is laid down. Another plus point is that a replaceable blade is available, but this should not be required until you have cut several hundreds of shanks. It will even cut through 3–4in (7.5–10cm) block sticks with ease. If cutting holly or thorn shanks, a pair of secateurs are a necessity for trimming afterwards.

2 Tools and Equipment

In stickmaking, as with most other crafts, you can indulge yourself with all sorts of tools, mechanical or otherwise, depending upon the depth of your pocket and just how sophisticated you wish to be. However, there are no tools made specifically for stickmaking and one must make do with existing equipment or use common sense and ingenuity in overcoming the problems that arise. A while ago I met two stickmakers in a week, both had horn-handled leaping trout sticks. Neither had many tools or much equipment to speak of, not even a vice, nor did they have workshops. One had heated the horn over the ring of a gas stove then ran outside and stuck one end into a small hole in the backyard stone wall, bent the horn roughly into shape and held it until set (at least ten minutes). The other had heated the horn over a little portable picnic stove on the kitchen table then hurried out into the garden and held the horn roughly in shape by clamping it to the top of the garden fence with a few G-cramps. Whilst neither stick would have any hope of being a show winner, they were very presentable sticks and one can only admire the makers' determination in adversity. A workshop is naturally a great asset if you have one but I know dozens of good stickmakers who do not.

Several use the kitchen table; some use a portable Workmate set up in the kitchen; others work in the garage, in the loft, a spare bedroom, a cellar, even in the cupboard under the stairs – and some are show winners.

Assuming that you have a workshop, or

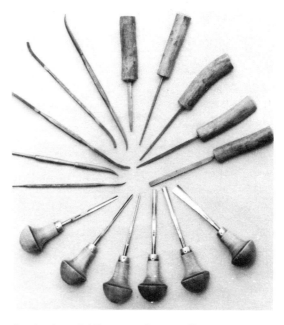

A selection of rifflers, needle rasps (for which handles have been made from reindeer antler) and small gouges. All are invaluable for carving.

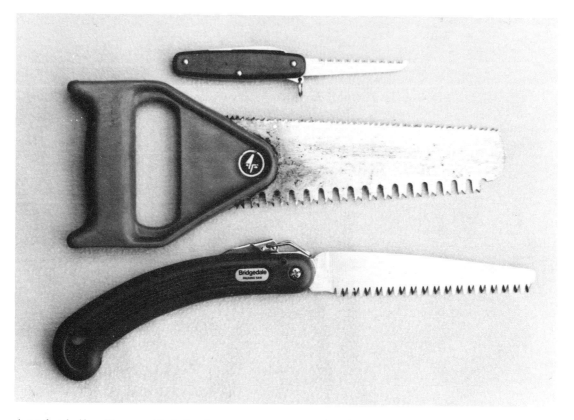

A pocket-knife with a saw blade is adequate to cut an occasional stick. The two-sided pruning saw will soon become blunt. A Japanese folding pruning saw is ideal for stick cutting.

at the least a work-bench, the first requirement is a vice, or better still two. Your first choice should be a bench or engineer's vice, which stands up from the bench on a base, and the other a carpenter's vice, preferably wide jawed, which stands flush with the work-top. Either will be costly if bought new (although those made in Taiwan or other Far Eastern countries are considerably cheaper), but both can often be picked up quite cheaply at car boot or jumble sales, Oxfam shops, and the type of junk and antique shops that stock tools, etc. The small advertisements in shop windows or local newspapers are also fruitful places to search.

Next in importance I would put a selection of wood rasps, flat, round and half round; fine cut, rough or medium. For years I got along happily with a flat and round Surform, then they brought out a half-round version and now that is a favourite, although I frequently use the other kinds as well. A tenon-saw, with its rigid blade, is ideal for cutting straight edges, whilst a carpenter's bow-saw, with its adjustable blade, cuts curves. A coping saw is useful, so is a small wood saw with a 6in (15cm) replaceable blade that fits in a frame. A selection of chisels and gouges is useful too but it is surprising how often a good sharp pocket-knife can do instead. A

A selection of lock knives. The prices vary greatly from the standard model on the left to the two very expensive models on the right.

knife is always better if it has a lock blade which prevents the blade from closing on your fingers accidentally. Knives can be bought in various sizes to suit all hands. You should be able to obtain one made from old-fashioned tool steel with a comfortable wood handle, that holds a good edge and sharpens easily on either oilstone or steel, for a minimal cost. The really up-market makes are expensive, owing to the quality of the steel used and their ability to hold their edge, but they will last you a lifetime.

Power tools and accessories certainly make life easier. Most handymen will already own an electric drill, complete with sanding discs. I never use paperbacked sanding discs, preferring the fibrebacked ones made for angle grinders because these do not clog too easily and have a very long life. Apart from ordinary twist drills, I have several flat bits or spade bits, which I use in the power tool for drilling out handles to take dowels. These have a long life as well and are easily sharpened as the cutting edges are simply the flat shoulders of the drill head. Flap wheels, a fairly recent innovation, are a great help for shaping inside curves. But by far the most useful power tool for the stickmaker is the Black and Decker Powerfile; as far as I know, no other manufacturer has yet produced anything similar. This is simply a short, fairly narrow arm around which passes a sanding belt on rollers. This is invaluable for shaping wood, horn or antler and is easily handled and extremely manoeuvrable. It is one of those tools which very quickly becomes indispensable. Nowadays the hot-air gun or paint stripper appears to be overtaking the naked flame appliances for the heating of horn. Certainly, it is slower to heat than, for example, a blowlamp but is not as liable to burn the horn – although it can do so if left playing on one spot too long.

Miniature power tools have their devotees. A useful accessory is a flexi-shaft for fine detailed work but as most of these tools can be held comfortably, pencil fashion, in the hand I feel that it is not really

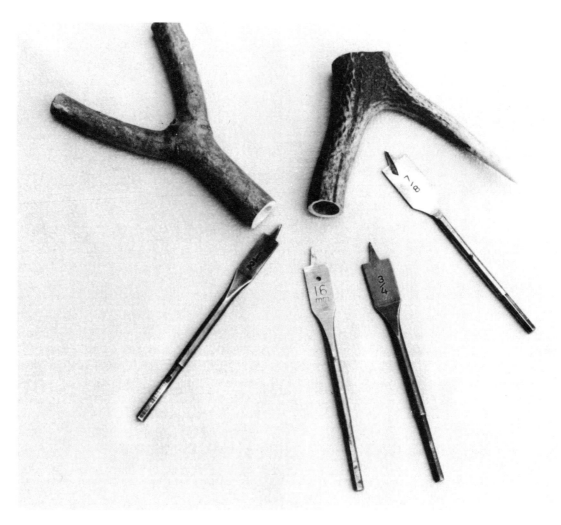

Flat bit drills, invaluable when dowelling.

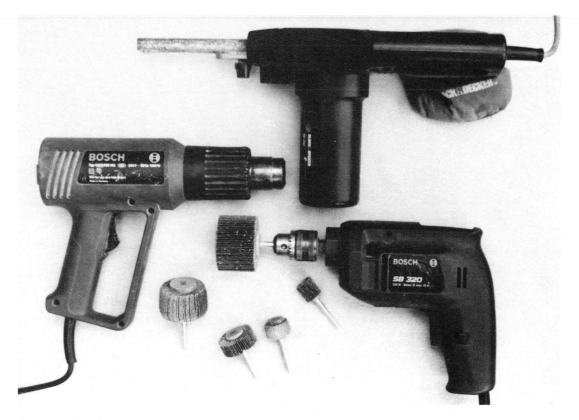

Power tools make life easier. A powerfile (top) is indispensable; a hot-air gun (left) is ideal for heating horn; flap wheels in a drill (right) make sanding and shaping inside curves easier.

essential. Numerous accessories are available: drills, burrs, drum sanders, flap wheels, etc but none are cheap. Ask your dentist to keep his used drills and burrs; although not new they are of better quality than the others.

I would consider a band-saw to be a luxury as you only seldom have a use for it. I have always managed without one. In fact, I know several stickmakers who dispense with all power tools and use hand tools only. One does all his carving using several needle files and rifflers, and another carves only with a knife, and they are both show winners.

A useful accessory is a pyrography kit.

This is a burning tool – virtually an electric soldering iron, but with a variety of shaped bits which can create feathers and fish scales, texture animal fur, burn in eyes and nostrils and have numerous other applications. It is first-class with wood and with antler which has been buffed down to the 'bone', but needs careful handling with horn as the heat tends to melt it, which rather softens the intended effect.

As you progress in stickmaking, you will find that you design and acquire various jigs and formers, templates, clamps and cramps. Most will have to be adapted for a particular task, say shaping a horn head. In horn bending a sash cramp

19

is essential, for instance. If it has those little round jaws which always slide off the object you wish to hold, have a small plate of mild steel, around 2in sq (5cm sq) welded on, and for holding horn a 1½in (3.8cm) long piece of pipe cut down the centre can be welded on to the fixed jaw. There is a sort of Parkinson's law of stick-making which rules that the bulk of tools and equipment will proliferate to fill the available workspace. I managed happily for years in an 8 × 6ft (2.4 × 1.8m) store-room, but now I have a 10 × 8ft (3 × 2.4m) shed, nearly twice as large, and it is just as crowded.

Abrasives are always needed and for the coarser grades I always use emery cloth rather than paper, which tears easily. Wet and dry is ideal for the finer grades for finishing and you will need successively finer grits up to 400 or even 600 to eliminate all hair-line scratches on horn. Use the abrasive backed by a cork block which will not groove the piece you are sanding down. For inside curves, use a round dowel-shaped length of dog chew wrapped around with emery. I also have several sanding blocks and dowels of different grades of emery which are tacked to the wood backing with a layer of firm foam rubber between. For finer work I often find that emery boards are useful. For general rounding of inside curves or thinning down a hand-piece overall there is nothing better than strapping (strips of emery cloth normally ½–1in (1.3–2.5cm) wide). If at all possible, try to obtain industrial grade of any type of abrasive, this being infinitely superior to the DIY types available. Steel wool (coarse grade) is useful for the removal of loose bark or 'dandruff' on shanks.

It is best to experiment before deciding on one method of colouring fancy sticks. Norman Tulip, the famous Northumbrian stick dresser, has never used anything but inks on his sticks. He tells me that he can obtain virtually any colour he requires by mixing shades and that inks are the easiest for this. I know stickmakers who use a children's painting set of water colours, and others who have an extensive – and expensive – selection of oils. Quite a few use felt-tip pens and, as these come in a comprehensive colour range nowadays, excellent results can be obtained. In the last few years more and more stickmakers have turned to acrylics but I have to say that, although in the hands of an expert this medium could not be bettered, quite a few efforts that I have seen have been abysmal; a pillar box red fox and a rich chestnut-coloured curlew come to mind. It is unfortunate that not all good stick-makers are good painters and that some of their efforts in this field do not complement their other skills. As well as bright primary colours, more subtle intermediate shades occur in nature and it is these which often elude them. A badger, for instance, is usually depicted in stark black and white whereas, in reality, the coat is made up of more sober shades of grey.

3 One-Piece Sticks

KNOB STICK

A knob stick is basically a shank with a piece of extra wood on the end, shaped in a knob which is usually sawn from the thicker branch, trunk or root from which the shank is growing. Normally only a very basic stick can be fashioned from these but the odd one gives promise of something better. A blackthorn knob, for instance, lends itself to a traditional Irish carved head. It is easy to whittle or carve and gives character to what would otherwise be an unremarkable stick. Certain dogs' heads and owls can also be fashioned from a knob stick but you will need a certain facility in carving to make a really good one.

THUMB STICK

A good one-piece thumb stick, with a well-balanced shank and symmetrical fork, is a rare find indeed. The balance is nearly always upset as any taper is the wrong way round, running up towards the handle. Also, the fork is often too narrow for comfort, and one which has been widened by bark and wood removal to accommodate the thumb is not a very pleasing sight.

Of all sticks, the thumb stick probably requires the least work to make it acceptable – there may be an odd twig or two (occasionally sprouting from the centre of the fork) to be removed, the arms of the fork to be levelled and rounded off or a little tidying up and perhaps straightening of the shank, and it is ready for work.

BLOCK STICK

This is a shank growing from a branch, trunk or large root from which a block of wood can be cut large enough to enable a crook or other handle to be carved. Hazel is the commonest type to be found but suitable holly and ash can also be had.

One ambition of mine had long been to make a blackthorn crook from such a block and during thirty years I just managed to find two. One was on the small side and it also cracked badly in the block when seasoning because I had forgotten to seal the cut edge. I ended up with a basic straight handle instead of a crook. However, the other one made a much cherished stick.

Block sticks are discussed in further detail in Chapter 4.

HONEYSUCKLE TWIST

Honeysuckle twines itself clockwise around the stem and branches of bushes and trees and, growing with the host plant, bites into the bark and will often distort the stem into a distinctive twist or spiral. Stickmakers usually prize a shank shaped in this way which can be found most commonly on hazel and ash. One big drawback to a 'twisty' stick is that somewhere along its length, and usually disguised by overgrown bark, there is often a weak spot where the honeysuckle bine has bitten in rather deeply. The spiral can be induced artificially by twining growing shanks at an early stage in their growth with nylon or other strong cord but you need patience – and well-hidden shanks, as stickmakers are a sharp-eyed lot!

CARVED-HANDLE STICK

When stick cutting, try to include some shanks with a length of branch or trunk attached, even if only the same diameter as the shank. These can often be shaped or carved into simple heads, depending not only on the size of the available wood but also on the imagination and skill of the carver. Certain dogs come to mind, usually with drop ears as stand-up ears in wood are vulnerable to damage. Labradors,

A scrapbook is invaluable for carving projects.

hounds, lurchers and certain terriers are ideal but unless you own one who will act as a model, obtain illustrations of both profile and front view before starting. A duck's head is a good curvaceous subject and badgers, stoats or weasels are not too difficult. It is advisable to keep a scrap-book of pictures of suitable subjects and try to obtain as many different angles as possible. The classic example is the duck's head which, in profile, is billiard ball round but from the front, a different shape entirely is seen, with a narrow crown which is only half the width of the lower part of the head. There is also a distinctive eye groove which runs approximately three-quarters the length of the head up to the bill.

Occasionally two lengths of branch can be obtained attached to a shank and very unusual fancy handles can be made. The one I most admired was a simply carved rabbit's head with the ears shaped from a pair of branches growing at just the right angle. I have also seen a stick with a T-shaped cross-piece handle carved as two ducks back-to-back, and another along the same lines with a hound and terrier.

ROOT STICK

A common countryman's stick is the root ash with a sturdy handle at right angles to the shank. These can occasionally be found by digging out a suitable shank which is growing on its own rootstock and finding a suitable root, but the majority are grown artificially. Two-year-old ash seed-lings, from a nursery, trimmed back to a suitable bud, are laid in a shallow trench and lightly covered with soil. The bud will develop vertically as a straight stem at right angles to the original stem which becomes the rootstock and eventually forms a natural handle. I have never seen holly or hazel in this style as both grow shoots from the parent bush or tree, but blackthorn grows from root suckers underground and can often be found with a suitable handle. The snag is that the main stem, which is to be used as the shank, is often devoid of spines, thus losing part of its attraction.

The main thing to remember when stick cutting is that you are not just seeking plain shanks. 'Eyeball' the length of each shank and often you will see a thumb piece that might otherwise have been over-looked, or a hazel piece from a branch, suitable for carving or even a block stick, and don't forget the piece that you can't see – the root. It is also a good idea, if practical, to view shanks from different angles. Hidden flaws often appear – badly damaged bark caused by chafing, bad kinks or dog-legs or even a drastic taper – not visible from other viewpoints.

BENT-HANDLE STICK

It is easy enough to make a wood crook or walking stick by heating 12–15in (30–37.5cm) from the end of a long shank. This can be done by devising a method of steaming using a kettle, tubing and some sort of bag, box or pipe. A sand-box can also be used – damp sand is heated and the end of the stick plunged into it for the required length of time. Another method is by softening with a hot-air gun, paint stripper or even a hair dryer. The softened part is then bent to a wood crook shape over a former and tied into position until set.

When set, the notch made initially near the end of the stick, to facilitate tying to the former when bent into shape, can be rounded out to give the 'nose out' crook shape, or the last 2in (5cm) of the handle can be re-heated and bent out at an angle to form the nose by slipping a piece of piping of suitable diameter over the end of it. The woods normally used for bending are ash and sweet chestnut, almost always coppice grown for the purpose. Hazel does not lend itself well to the bending process as the bark peels too readily and it is also prone to splitting under pressure, while holly and blackthorn are prized too highly to be subjected to this treatment.

There are, however, three main drawbacks to all these bending methods – or rather with the results they produce. All treated sticks will have deep wrinkles under the curve of the crown where the bark has folded in on itself in the shaping of the handle. All will also have stretch marks and invariably cracked bark and often broken fibres across the top of the crown. When smoothed down, these imperfections make the diameter of the handle at the curve of the crown narrower than the remainder of the stick and will result in a flat instead of a round shape in the handle. The main fault is, without doubt, the lack of stability in the handle shape. Go out in the rain carrying one of these sticks and leave it in a warm room afterwards or inadvertently lean it against a warm chimney-breast or radiator, and the handle will start losing its shape as the stretched curves slowly start to contract. The handle can of course be re-heated and coaxed back into shape but there will always be that inexorable tendency to warp which is inherent in this type of stick. Many stickmakers decide to make a stick or two of this type at some stage but I doubt that any of them feel lasting satisfaction with the results achieved.

4 Block Sticks

My advice to any stickmaker would always be to forget about bending a handle and to make instead a crook or market stick from a block stick. Hazel is most commonly used for block sticks but holly, ash, hawthorn and blackthorn are stronger, and I would certainly have the latter every time. When cutting shanks you will occasionally see one growing from a suitable branch or trunk. An ideal block would be 3–5in (7.5–12.5cm) in diameter with the stick growing from it at an angle of not more than 45 degrees. Saw off this block (undercut first to save splitting or pulling off a heel) about 2in (5cm) above the join and 4–6in below it. As soon as possible, seal the cut ends of the block with two coats of knotting (knot sealer) or melted candle wax. Then, to speed up seasoning, I take off strips of bark longitudinally from the block with a sharp knife or axe. Using this method the block will season in about half the time it would normally take.

When seasoned, take off the rest of the bark from the block, being careful not to overrun on to the shank. The block will now require to be sawn or rasped flat on each side, leaving a plank thickness of about 1¼in (3.2cm) which should be in line with the shank. I usually slip a length of hose up the shank towards the joint with

the block, when sawing, to prevent accidental damage to the shank. If the shank is out of line with the block, heat near the joint gently with a blowlamp or hot-air gun, then clamp the block horizontally in

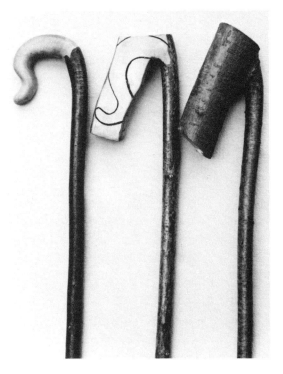

A wood crook from a block stick: (right to left) the block as cut; seasoned, planked and crook marked out; complete.

a vice with a rubber wedge easing the shank into line. The setting period can be speeded up by spraying with cold water.

The overall shape of the handle can now be determined, allowing for the restrictions presented by the block size and its angle to the shank. I normally draw the outline free-hand on the block with a felt-tipped pen or biro, following up the line of the shank from the join, but I also have a set of templates cut from semi-rigid, clear plastic sheet. These can give a good idea of a suitable shape and also enable the use of any interesting grain or figuration present in the block.

Once a suitable handle has been decided on, the cutting out of the block can be undertaken. When cutting out, always leave the proposed handle thicker than what will eventually be required as it is best to have a safety margin. A band-saw is obviously the easiest method of cutting out but I have never been fortunate enough to have had access to one. I have always used an old-fashioned carpenter's bow-saw where both handles can be twisted to allow the cutting angle of the blade to be changed. The shape could be cut out by use of various rasps, a round and half-round Surform being particularly useful. At this stage it is not necessary to work to any fine tolerance and a crude overall shape is all that is required. Any surplus wood at the heel, crown and nose is next sawn off and a round rasp used to shape the nose if a crook is planned.

The overall shape should now be apparent and, using sanding blocks, rasps, etc., take off any sharp edges left by the saw. Shaping the underside of the curve of the crown and nose is usually left till last, being the most difficult part, but the use of round and half-round rasps usually eases the task. Finish off by strapping with emery cloth, starting with a coarse grade (40 grit perhaps), and followed with increasingly finer grades to ensure a smooth finish. Try to feather down the bark at the top of the shank where it turns around the crown to form the heel. Look at the handle from different angles frequently and always ensure that the handle is in line with the shank. While it is all very well for a horn-handled stick to have a nice taper down to a slender nose, this will not do for a wood stick where a thin nose would be vulnerable to breakage. Allow a slight taper towards the nose but try to retain a general overall strength in the handle.

Hold the handle up to the light regularly so that any scratch-marks or flat planes can be seen and rectified. When you feel that you have finally smoothed the whole handle down ready for polishing, rub in a little coffee stain and you will see just how many scratches you have missed! Some parts of the block will obstinately refuse to be smoothed down and will retain a fuzzy, slightly rough finish in the grain. Wet these areas with a damp cloth, which will raise the grain even further, then singe lightly with your blowlamp, hot-air gun or candle. The whiskers on the slightly singed part can then be sanded down and the rough spot should have vanished. There may be a piece of ingrown bark, knot-hole or other flaw in the wood but, as long as these do not run too deep, it is an easy matter to scoop them out with a knife point or suitable gouge until sound wood is reached. The resulting hole can be camouflaged by filling with clear resin casting liquid which makes a nearly invisible repair. Wood dust mixed with glue to create a stiff paste can also be used but a good colour match is difficult as the glue usually discolours the dust.

A water stain, caused by rain collecting

in the hollow created by the angle at which the shank grew from the block, may also occur, but this will often add to the appeal of a nicely shaped handle. I have also seen in blackthorn blocks a very striking purplish stain running through the wood. This stain is always present in the bark and it appears that it can sometimes run through into the grain of the wood. Blackthorn block sticks are rare in any event so it may well be that this colouring is common in this timber.

A thin block that runs virtually parallel to the shank seems to be an unlikely subject for a crook but, in fact, it often lends itself to the making of a leg crook or cleek style. By tradition, the dimensions of this crook were an old penny in diameter for the inside of the crown and an old half-penny in diameter across the mouth. As these crooks were meant purely as a practical shepherd's tool for a particular breed of sheep, it is not essential that these measurements are now strictly adhered to. When I make this style of stick I like to be able to grip the handle comfortably without rubbing the backs of my fingers against the inside of the nose. This style has a more elongated nose than the standard crook shape and it is essential not to weaken it by thinning it down too much. A good, well-shaped leg cleek, in either wood or horn, has in fact very little taper towards the nose.

Whatever wood is used, grain direction is all important. A block stick can be fashioned with a classic crook shape but if the grain in the crown is running parallel to the shank there will be a potential weak spot in the short grain. I would treat this sort of stick with respect as frequent handling and the inevitable bumps or knocks will almost certainly result in a clean break across the crown. This is unlikely to happen where the grain direction runs along the length of the handle as this should be a very strong, practical stick.

THE HALF STICK

Whilst a repair could be made if there is a break across the crown, the join would never be invisible and there would always be the fear that a further break could occur elsewhere. It is better by far, if there is about 2in (5cm) of the crown remaining attached to the shank, to use this as a basis for a half stick. This type of stick originates in the North. It consists of a shank which has no more than half of the crown of a

A half stick made from ash and buffalo horn.

27

handle attached, and to this has been added the remainder of the crown and the nose (usually in the market stick nose-in style) in horn or occasionally antler. I would imagine that this sort of stick started life because of the weak spot in crooks where there is short grain across the crown, and broke off, or it may just have been that some canny countryman decided that a good shank with the beginnings of a handle coming away along the crown had the makings of something more than just a shank. An extension in horn was added and a new type of stick came into being. It can be very attractive and, being fairly simple to make, is one way to utilize a short length of horn or shank with a part crown that is too small to offer scope for anything else.

The horn must be at least 5–6in (12.5–15cm) long and should be heated and shaped to a suitable angle. The dimensions of the base should be greater than the end of the wood crown and both must be cut off at the correct angle to enable a good clean joint to be made. The strongest type of joint is made by drilling out the base of the horn and fashioning a dowel to match on the crown but a commercial dowel or length of studding could also be used. The most difficult problem is getting the extension to sit properly and greater scope is provided in shaping up after jointing if the horn is rather thicker than required and can be bevelled down accordingly afterwards. Cow horn, with its rich colouring, probably gives the best results although both coloured and black buffalo can also look good but I find that ram's horn does not team up quite so well except perhaps with a darker type of shank such as blackthorn or a deep brown hazel. The stick might well be a triumph of improvization but it can more than hold its own in what might be thought more select company.

5 Wood Handles

Block sticks are not easy to come by. I manage to cut perhaps one for every hundred shanks obtained, and even then it isn't always a good one. But there is a way to obtain blocks fairly easily, and as you will have a good choice you can afford to be selective and only cut good ones. When out cutting, keep a look out for a suitable block with a short length of shank – 4in (10cm) is sufficient – coming away from it at a good angle. This can be seasoned and then jointed to a matching shank (after cutting out the handle from the block) to make a wood crook. I have made several blackthorn and holly block sticks this way over the years and, in my opinion, they equal the one-piece block stick. You can quite often actually improve the looks of the sticks by having an antler spacer or collar between handle and shank, thus emphasizing the two-piece nature of the stick, but, of course, you would not be able to enter such sticks in shows where one-piece crooks are specified.

Even if the blocks that I have come across are not large enough to create a crook, as long as they have a length of shank growing from them, with a suitable diameter (normally around 1in/2.5cm) I will cut them, as they lend themselves to other types of handles. A good walking stick handle, perhaps with in-curved nose, can be made from a block with a shank piece at right angles. Heads of dogs, birds, animals, sometimes even fish, are possibilities, given a block of the right shape, and a minimum of skill. Quite often you will sense that a certain piece is ideal for something but you are not quite sure what, until someone else sees it and remarks that it looks like an owl or a weasel, or whatever. Children are particularly good at this, perhaps because they are more imaginative.

I always look out for likely handles and have a box full of them in my workshop. It

Suitable handles that require minimal shaping.

is surprising how often that I can remember cutting a certain shaped piece, even after several years, and seek it out for the stick that I am working on. Never ignore a natural even-sided fork – the kind that would make a good catapult – because, fitted to a good long shank, these will invariably produce a better thumb stick than the one-piece variety, where the fork is not always symmetrical and the shank invariably thickens towards the base, leaving the stick badly balanced. Similarly, a 6in (15cm) length of honeysuckle twist, with well-defined spirals, jointed to a matching shank, with perhaps just a sliver of polished horn atop of the handle, can more than hold its own with most twisty shanks with the almost inevitable bark-hidden weak spot somewhere along the length. Some woods, such as blackthorn, will produce a fair number of handle pieces for plain walking sticks consisting of branches which grow away at right angles somewhere along their length. Cut off the L-shaped section, with each arm 4–5in (10–12.5cm) long and there is your handle. Simply fit to a matching shank and round off the knuckle and the nose; or countersink an old copper wren farthing in the nose – when polished this makes a very nice feature.

Not every kind of wood is suitable for handles. Lime is probably the carver's favourite wood, being easily worked and with a nice pale colour which polishes well. However, it is too soft for handles, and dents or breaks easily. Beech is attractive but is too evenly grained to be interesting and has little colour variation or figuring along its length; it also shatters readily across a short-grain section. Nowadays, one sees pieces of elm board bearing a template drawing of a crook handle or the handle already cut out by a band-saw. The red-brown timber looks very tempting but resist the lure, as the timber will be fairly straight grained and weak across the crown. Try, instead, to obtain a piece of burr elm which will be much stronger and almost certainly more attractive. For the same reasons, I would not use birch unless it was a burr piece.

Some of the nicest wood can come from the unlikeliest sources. Yew is always associated with churchyards although it can be found in the wild, and is often cut back if overhanging a field, as the leaves are poisonous to livestock. Thus, good pieces of this very rich-coloured timber can be obtained quite often and they can make beautiful handles. It probably has more colour variation that any other native timber, has a close, even grain and fine figuring which takes a good finish and polish and so is well worth looking out for. Juniper, a common shrub of high ground in northern Britain, is very similar. Laburnum is a favourite in older gardens and again good pieces can be had when being cut back. The wood will often have a green shade, making it very distinctive and a well-marked figure. The commonest shrub in parks is usually laurel and, as it is a natural sprawler, it needs regular attention. This wood is rather similiar to walnut, varying from light brown to brownish black and has the desired stickmaking virtues, being strong, tough and durable. The trimmings will usually end up on the bonfire so it pays to have a word with the park gardeners who will be only too pleased to have it taken off their hands and will, no doubt, keep any other likely timber for you.

I received a nice present while in the Cotswolds a few years back: a large broken-off, and partly seasoned, branch from a walnut tree in the garden of our holiday cottage. The botanical name for walnut (*Regia*) means 'fit for a King', which describes the timber well. Light-brown to nearly black, it is smooth, hard, tough, stable and shock resistant – and extremely attractive. Sporting gun stocks are traditionally made from walnut and I was very pleased to be given a broken one recently from the local gunshop. This made some lovely handles but, because of the very rich colouration of the timber, care must be taken in deciding on suitable subjects if birds or animals are to be carved; a badger, for instance, would be inappropriate.

Most good timber merchants will have a comprehensive stock of seasoned native timber, assuming that you are unable to find your own. This is usually ready-planked and planed on one side to show grain and colour and, although you may feel that some are expensive, remember that a yard-long board, 6in (15cm) wide and preferably slightly thicker than 1in, will yield half a dozen crooks and possibly one or two thumb pieces as well. Even if you have nothing particular in mind, a visit to such an establishment is an education, and rarely will you leave empty handed! Apart from home-grown timbers, you may well be attracted towards some of the foreign woods on display. Several of them can make excellent handles and indeed complete sticks, but I can not really say that I care for the 'billiard cue' type of shank produced. The following are useful woods for handles:

African Blackwood Very hard, dense and heavy. An unusual dark black/brown in colour. Striking when made up with a light-coloured shank or a stripped holly.
Bubinga Purplish-brown to deep crimson; well figured with bands and a mottled or marbled effect. Strong and hard.

Indian Laurel Similar to the home-grown variety but rather more richly coloured.
Lignum Vitae Heaviest, hardest, and most close-grained of all timbers. Very distinctive greenish-black colour with well defined bands of light and dark brown running longitudinally. Excellent for a thumb stick. Has an oily finish and will not take varnish.
Purple Heart Really *is* purple, but will fade (like teak) to a silver-grey shade with exposure, unless protected with linseed oil.
Rosewood Several varieties, mainly South American in origin. Expensive. One of the most beautiful of all timbers. Dark-brown/red to purple in colour, richly figured and giving an exceptionally smooth finish. Makes very pleasing handles indeed.
American Black Walnut Distinctive colour; deep chocolate brown which can have a violet-purple tinge. A good piece will make a very luxurious handle.

It is advisable to wear a face mask when working these timbers as their dusts can be harmful.

If you intend to do fancy carving on a handle, I always think that it is nicer to be able to achieve your object without recourse to painting. The wood used has a great bearing on this. Holly and hazel, for instance, are both very light coloured and their looks improve immeasurably with a light coffee stain. Ash, blackthorn, rowan and hawthorn do not need this treatment, although all will look better after one or two applications of linseed oil, as will oak, elm, and the fruit-woods. Yew, juniper, and walnut are all richly coloured and figured and for this reason need to be used with discretion. I have seen professionally carved, walnut stick heads of dogs, badgers, foxes, trout, pheasants, ducks, curlews, otters and weasels, from broken gun stocks. They were all lovingly carved, but the wood, beautiful as it was, simply did not do justice to some of the subjects. The badgers and the curlews in particular, and one or two of the others just did not look right.

It is sometimes necessary to paint wood when depicting brightly coloured birds – blue tits or jays, for instance. Others, which are readily identifiable, such as woodpeckers or kingfishers with their distinctive beaks, do not really require colour to take the eye. A fox head in just the right shade of russet, in juniper, yew or elm, can be stunning, and most brownish birds (wrens, curlews, mallard ducks and hen pheasants) can be quite accurately depicted using coffee stain. Feather markings can be emphasized by the light use of a gouge or chisel which creates flecks or crescent shapes that always look darker than the rest of the wood when stained.

There are some very skilled carvers around in the stickmaking world but they are not all good stickmakers. It seems to me that they have looked upon the carving project in isolation without visualizing it attached to the shank with the whole coming together harmoniously. Their carving is purely an appendage either to a shank or a handle with no concessions made to the handling or the feel of the stick. A good stick should always 'come to the hand', a saying which is self-explanatory. Such sticks look good, feel comfortable in the hand and are well balanced. The other kind, with a growth in the form of a carving, either comprising the actual handle itself or from that part of the handle where your hand naturally grips, never feel right. After all, a handle is meant to be handled! To give but one example of such sticks (and they can be seen at all stick shows), I can remember a lovely little carving of a full-bodied duck about 2–3in (5–7.5cm) long. This had been fixed to a shank by the middle of its body which meant, naturally, that the stick could only be gripped below the handle, which is rather ridiculous when you think about it. If I carved such objects myself I would never dream of fitting them to shanks and calling them sticks, although I would be very gratified to have them on a display shelf at home. Fancy sticks, such as the one described, are never used as a rule, being meant for shows, or perhaps as a wall or hall-stand decoration. Apart from anything else, they would lose beaks, tails and heads in quick succession if handled as ordinary sticks. Subjects that can be safely carved in antler or horn, which has much greater strength, should not really be attempted in wood – the curlew being a good example.

6 Burrs

A burr in wood is an aberration in normal growth where the grain and figuration of the timber becomes distorted. This fault is advantageous for stickmaking, and is particularly desirable for crooks and market sticks because a straight grain should be avoided when making handles (thumb sticks excepted) – cutting out the shape of the crown will result in a short-grain pattern with its inherent weakness. The grain in a burr is tangled and intertwined and naturally stronger. It may show an attractive 'bird's eye' pattern, sometimes quite extensively, which will make a very nice handle indeed. A burr will also change the colour of the timber in a few instances, particularly with some elm, which can have a deep, rich mahogany-red shade in place of the usual brown. Burr oak will also tend to be a much richer shade of brown than the normal wood.

I do not recollect ever having seen burrs on hazel but I have come across them on holly and, occasionally, on overgrown hawthorn trees, so they may also occur on the trunks of old blackthorn. It is quite common to see them on elm, oak, birch and on all fruitwood timber – apple, cherry, damson, plum and pear. On ash, they even grow down to the base of the trunk.

Usually there are only one or two burrs on the affected tree, appearing as rounded swellings bulging from the trunk, but some trees are covered with them – I

A burr on a silver birch trunk.

counted upwards of thirty on an old birch once. An average size would be about 2ft (60cm) across. If you want to cut a burr, saw down the length of the trunk, not across it. If it can be done without felling the tree, all the better – there may be another in the same place in a few years time. You will need a thickness of at least 2–3in (5–7.5cm) as the bark is usually deeply fissured, cracked and encrusted, and a depth of 1in (2.5cm) may have to be removed before the timber is reached. Season in the normal way, with plenty of air circulating, but keep out of the sun and turn the wood occasionally to prevent curling. It is advisable to seal with knotting to lessen the risk of checking.

When seasoned, the handle shape is often dictated more by the characteristics than by its size. I would not recommend the use of rasps, apart from fine ones, when working the burr, as some parts are exceptionally hard and cause snagging, which results in pieces being ripped out. The final finishing, using abrasives, can be frustrating as a smooth surface seems to be very elusive, the one consolation being that minor scratches do not show up readily. I like to rub on a little linseed oil in the later stages, when any obstinate fuzzy patches can be identified. The wood will almost always be pock-marked, pin-holed

A burr on the end of a cherry branch.

and sometimes covered with characteristic small crescent-shaped splits. Often, there will be pieces of ingrown bark which I usually remove; if they are too deeply ingrained, only take off the top, leaving a shallow depression. These faults can be almost invisibly repaired or disguised by filling any depressions with glue, sprinkling on fine sawdust obtained from the timber, and smoothing down when the glue is set. Alternatively, experiment (as turners sometimes do when making bowls) with a filler in a contrasting colour to the timber, using either paint or fabric dye in powder form mixed with the glue. You might even want to try the rather exotic idea of using brass or copper dust (easily obtained by fine-sanding a piece of the chosen piping over a sheet of paper) in the glue. This is quite striking on the darker burrs, particularly those which are well pock-marked.

There is also a growth which looks like a miniature burr, which is actually a gall produced by insect activity. Oak seems particularly prone to them but they can also be found on holly, hawthorn, ash and cherry, producing a swelling from about the size of a golf ball up to those with a diameter of 3–4in (7.5–10cm). Sometimes it is possible to lever these off the tree trunk without sawing. The bark can be smooth or deformed as with a burr and, when removed, will usually show a very striking grain and figure. The wood will often have an unusual green tinge to it. Obviously their size limits their uses, but they make exceptional knob handles. Certain dogs' heads can be considered and with very little shaping you can create a very nice owl. There are no difficulties in finishing off and the wood will take a very fine polish.

I doubt if galls can be obtained from

Two handles can be cut from an expensive burr piece.

Oak galls and a typical handle.

timber merchants but most good ones will have a stock of burrs. They are more expensive than ordinary timber but well worth the effort in seeking out. It is a little confusing, when faced with an array of different timber, to find just what you want; as with bookshops, it pays to browse. It might also be advisable to take along some clear plastic templates of handles, which are a great help in weighing up the merits of a burr piece with bird's-eye patterning or nice figuring. Even card templates would give some indication of size and I never go to select timber without carrying a tape-measure or rule of some kind. A 6in sq (15cm sq) section that is marginally more than 1in (2.5cm) thick is more than adequate for a full crook and a good thumb stick requires no more than 4in × 3in (10cm × 7.5cm). Most firms will cut timber to order free of charge.

7 Deer Antler

Antler has been a favourite with stick-makers since at least Victorian times. It is reasonably easy to obtain, not too expensive, can be worked without any great effort and gives very pleasing results. Deer are increasing their numbers and extending their territory rapidly, even in the wild and inhospitable Scottish Highlands where a recent official estimate of the native red deer population gave a figure in excess of 300,000. There are four main species in Great Britain – red, fallow, roe and sika, the latter being the rarest. All have antler suitable for stickmaking. In addition there is a managed herd of reindeer at Glenmore near Aviemore on Speyside, and animals from here can now be seen in wildlife parks throughout the country.

Antler is bone and can not be shaped after heating, unlike horn. I have experimented over the years by boiling or heating with a blowlamp, a hot-air gun and even a microwave oven, and find that it will move fractionally (perhaps ¼–½in/ 0.6–1.3cm) but any more pressure will result in a fracture. It must be used as it stands, so consider the whole carefully before cutting to shape. With roe antler the options are limited because of its size (9in (23cm) overall being about the maximum). I always turn over an antler several times in my hands to see it from different angles before deciding where to cut, as often I find that one which at first seemed most suitable for a 'walker' handle would actually be better as a thumb stick piece.

The fertility of the soil in a particular area affects the quality of the grazing which in turn will influence the weight of

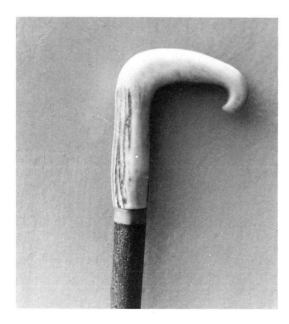

A sambar antler, which has little pith, made into a 'walker' handle.

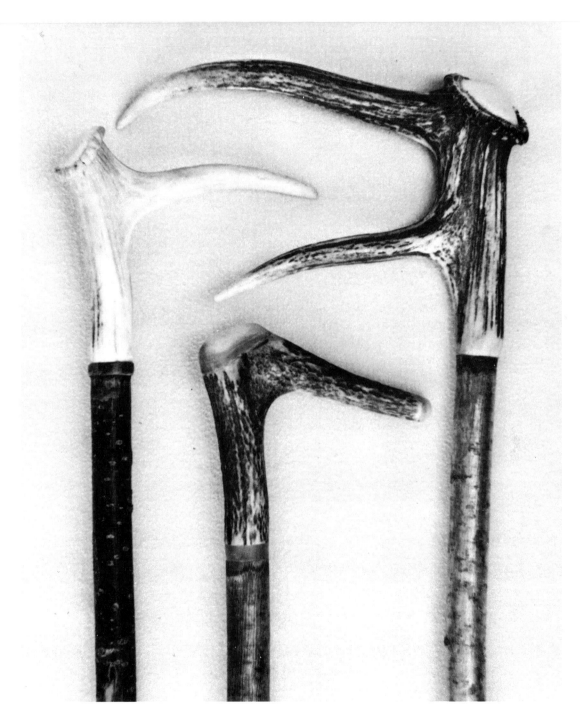

A coronet with a brow tine, a coronet with two adjacent tines and a 'walker' handle, horn capped on cut edges.

the antlers. Antlers of the same size may, therefore, vary greatly in weight. Age and health also affect growth and condition. A lightweight antler will be found to have a bigger pith running through the centre with just a thin horn covering, whereas a heavy one will have a smaller pith and correspondingly thicker horn. However, the strength of antler is considerable and there is little danger of damage occurring even with a lightweight piece when made up as a stick handle.

All deer cast their antlers annually – roe in late autumn and the others in the spring. Cast antler will have the coronet at one end, which is a girdle of rough, crusty wart-like segments. A handle which includes the coronet is always much admired and, if for sale, will be priced higher than handles fashioned from other parts of the antler, but they are very uncomfortable. This is particularly true of roe antler as this has rough nodules called pearling. A choice has to be made between looks and comfort.

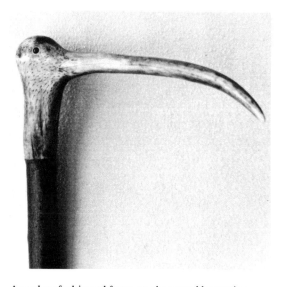

A curlew fashioned from an elongated brow tine.

TYPES OF ANTLER

Red

The red deer is by far the most common deer in Britain, there being well over 250,000 of them in Scotland alone. There are herds on Exmoor, in the Quantocks, the New Forest and in Lancashire, plus numerous others in parkland and on deer farms, which have proliferated in the last few years. By far the best antler for the stickmaker comes from Scotland as most from elsewhere are too bulky to be of much use. Antler from first- and second-year stags is to be preferred to that from older beasts for the same reason. Cast antler can be expected from about the end of March in Scotland, with the older stags casting before the young ones, but the antler is removed in the Autumn on deer farms to prevent damage while fighting. There is a considerable demand for antler for craft work and the days when you could get a sackful in exchange for a bottle of whisky are long gone. Antler is now sold by weight; you should get at least two or perhaps three fairly good antlers in a kilo. I usually obtain mine from stalking estates; locals will always know the location of the stalker's cottage. I always make them an offer of a stick, even if it can not be delivered until the following year!

The tines or points of red deer antler grow on one side, usually with a fork towards the tip. A good antler will have three tines of various shape and length, with a tip of either two or three points, and from this – if you are fortunate – you should be able to fashion four handles. These would be a coronet 'walker', two plain 'walkers', and a thumb stick, or two thumb sticks if one of the plain 'walkers' is inverted. You should aim to have at least

3in (7.5cm) for the neck of each handle. If you are not experienced with antler, mark each cut with biro beforehand. There is nothing worse than cutting off a piece only to realize that had you cut elsewhere you would have had a better shape or even an extra handle piece. Some tines are very long and need to be trimmed down but, again, do not be too hasty as occasionally one will suggest a beak (of a curlew, for example) and offer the possibility of a fancy handle. Conversely, an undeveloped brow tine – any length from ¼in (0.6cm) upwards – can suggest a nose and the basis for a face, particularly as the coronet can be the brow or hair-line. The rough end of the antler which the coronet encircles will need to be smoothed down and I always leave this dome shaped rather than flat. A monk or abbot's face can be simply carved, using the coronet as a tonsure.

The tines are often well spaced out and you can have a plain length of antler 4–5in (10–12.5cm) in length, and usually growing thicker in diameter, left over after cutting your handles. These off-cuts do not readily suggest a handle but if you shape four finger grooves along the inside edge and add a topping of horn, you will have a nice piece. Mark the grooves out initially with the edge of a coarse file roughly one inch (2.5cm) apart, open them up with a round rasp and finish with an emery-wrapped length of dowel. The horn topping sets the handle off nicely – simply cut roughly to shape, glue firmly in place and smooth down and polish when set. A variation on this style incorporates the coronet after removing the brow tine. After grooving as before, remove with a coping saw a 1in (2.5cm) portion of the coronet on the reverse side to the grooves. Bevel out a shallow groove in this cut-out

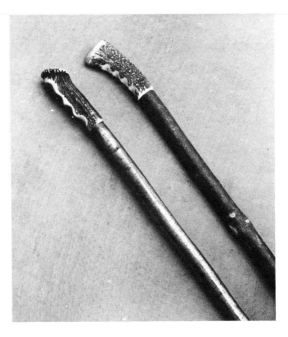

Antler finger-grooved handles. The coronet one also includes a thumb groove. The other is horn capped.

section to make a thumb rest and you have a five-finger grip handle. Mounted on a long sturdy shank this is a favourite with fishermen as a wading pole.

Any tines that are too long (more than 5in (12.5cm)) are normally cut off at that length and again, the appearance can be improved by a capping of horn on the cut face of the tine. A hand-piece which has been cut just above a tine will also benefit from a horn cap. I have seen this cap made from polished wood, such as walnut or mahogany, but this can not match horn for looks. Occasionally, a tine will be too thick and unwieldy to make anything other than a rather heavy and clumsy handle. But if the tine is approximately at right angles to the main stem of the antler and its diameter is 1in (2.5cm) or so when cut off at a length of around four inches (10cm), the tine can comprise the neck of the stick with the

A fox mask scrimshaw on an antler thumb stick.

if the coronet part of the antler is included. Finish off again with a horn cap on the cut edge of the handle. If a tine has sufficient diameter across a cut face I have occasionally countersunk an old wren farthing in it but you will require a surface of approximately one inch (2.5cm) for this as the farthing measures ¾in (2cm). The copper of the coin polishes up beautifully. Ensure that it is held firmly in place with glue, which can be mixed with wood or antler/horn dust to act as a filler to give the coin a flush fit if you have drilled too deeply.

The tip of the antler, with its two or three tines, is invariably made into thumb sticks. If there are three tines, there is normally a shallow cup-shaped depression in front of the centre tine which makes a comfortable thumb rest. The centre tine can, of course, be removed but this is usually for cosmetic purposes and rarely results in a better thumb hold. If the ridge between the tines of a thumbstick is too narrow for comfort this can be levelled out more with an emery-covered dowel. The points of all tines, which are normally smooth unlike the remainder of the antler, will benefit from buffing down with fine abrasives then polishing. I never like to see too sharp a point on any tine whether thumb stick or otherwise and either round them off more bluntly or cut and top with horn which is then polished. Very rarely will the tines be the same length and you will have to decide whether you want a 'natural' thumb stick, with perhaps one tine twice the length of the other, or the improved version with both tines cut to the same length and perhaps horn capped.

Sika

This Japanese species was not introduced into this country until the end of the last

main stem portion as the handle. The handle part will probably be too thick for comfort so should be sanded or rasped down, removing in the process all or most of the grooves in the antler. When finally polished, the resulting handle can closely resemble ivory and looks particularly nice century. Nowhere are they common; perhaps the best-known herds being in the New Forest and in parts of the Great Glen in Invernessshire. They are a very secretive woodland animal and unless you live in an area frequented by them (or are friendly with someone who does!) you will have difficulty in trying to obtain their antler. This is fairly similar to that of red deer but less inclined to curve along its length and with tines that come away at a sharp angle. It makes first-class thumb sticks. Probably the best way to try to obtain a supply would be through the Forestry Commission game rangers in the New Forest.

Roe

I think that I am correct in saying that roe are represented in every county in mainland Britain and are extremely common in some areas; I have seen nineteen in one field bordering woodland at Rothiemurchus by Aviemore on Speyside. They cast antler in late autumn and as they are in the main a woodland species it is seldom that you will find any. Yet they can be found; a farmer friend at Rothiemurchus told me that he once picked up five in one morning by the side of a fence in a field bordering a wood. He believes that the jarring caused by jumping the fence shakes loose the antler which is ready to be cast. Certainly the only two that I have ever found were by the side of fences.

Even if you have a source of supply, you will only occasionally get antler of stickmaking quality from northern Britain as the diameter is so small that you would be able to use a slender shank only. Roe antler is really only suitable for thumb sticks and even then you will not find one with a symmetrical shape as the three tines are never situated to give a classic Y. Care is needed in jointing to the shank if the coronet is to be retained as this will usually have a pronounced slant. Alternatively, the coronet can be removed but this is rarely done as the use of the complete antler always results in a more attractive stick. If you do not care for thumb sticks and provided that you have a substantial antler with a thickness of at least an inch (2.5cm), cut off the antler leaving 4 or 5in (10 or 12cm) including the coronet. Remove also the brow tine and you can shank from the opposite end to the coronet leaving you with a rather nice knob stick. The pearling on roe antler is usually very pronounced and sometimes very sharp edged and will need to be sanded down to remove the roughness. There is very little pith in roe antler.

Fallow

Fallow deer are the principal species to be kept in deer parks and apart from their

Roe antler that is only suitable for thumb sticks. These average 8–9in in length.

A fallow antler of which at least half is palmate and a red antler.

palmate antler are also notable for having four main colour variations: true fallow (a light fawnish red), black, white, and menil (spotted), with a further long-haired type in parts of Shropshire. They are common in the wild south of the Midlands but rare elsewhere. Being a woodland species and ranging over a wide area means that cast antler is not easily found. The Forestry Commission game rangers in Mortimer Forest in Shropshire, for instance, find very few cast antlers even though Fallow are common there. However, most Scots stalkers will find at least three-quarters of those cast by red stags on their estates.

Fallow antler has only a brow tine and one other and ends in a broad, curved palmate section which can be 6in (15cm) or more in width. The brow tine is usually heavily curved and will normally provide a nice coronet handle. The other tine is often too small to make a decent walker handle piece but should otherwise make a thumb stick. The palmated part is not very useful from the stickmaking angle and yet I am asked every year by the proprietor of a shooting and fishing type of shop in the Lake District to make up some of those 'daft sticks' as he always calls them. These consist of a normal shank surmounted by a palmated section of antler which looks decidedly incongruous. He tells me that he never has any trouble selling them but feels, as I do, that they are rarely if ever carried, being used instead to decorate hall-stands or fireplaces. The palmated part of the antler does not reach its full spread until the buck is at least seven years old and on younger animals might only be 2in (5cm) in width. A buck in his second year is known as a pricket; his antlers consist of a knobbly coronet and a single spike of a length of 2–6in (5–15cm). On odd occasions, one of these can be of sufficient width to provide a coronet knob handle.

Reindeer

The only herd of reindeer in the country is on Speyside near Aviemore, which consists of some eighty to ninety animals. They are a keeper managed herd but live wild on the Cairngorms and are not fenced in. They differ from other deer in that both male and female bear antlers and these are cast at any time from late autumn to spring. The antler is unusual in several respects. It is rarely grooved or striated as is normally the case and consequently, looking like bone, is not particularly attractive; It is rather pale in appearance, invariably curved along its length and lacks the characteristic pattern of tines of other deer antler; it is so randomly shaped that very few of the herd have similar antlers. Some unusual hand-pieces can therefore be made but you can rarely purchase a sufficient quantity to enable any selection to be made. There is little pith in the antler unless it is a young beast; this makes it rather heavy and any unused pieces can make excellent handles for knives, rasps, files, etc. Being fairly smooth it takes stain readily, although more than one application may be needed; permanganate of potash is particularly effective.

WORKING WITH ANTLER

The commonest problem facing novice stickmakers working with antler is always

A fox and rabbit scrimshaw on a fallow palmate antler makes a decorative but impractical stick.

what to do with the pith. This is simply answered: if pith is showing at the part to be jointed to the shank, try to remove as much as possible from the portion which the dowel is to fit into – I use a flat bit drill. It is not important if a rim of pith is left as the glue will adhere to this just as readily as it would to the antler. If there is a cut surface showing pith at the top of the handle or on the end of a trimmed tine, cap with a piece of horn, glued on and polished afterwards.

Antler varies in colour from deep brown to near white and a light-coloured handle always goes well with a dark shank and vice versa. Of course this is not a cardinal rule; handle and shank of roughly the same shade can look good if a white collar or spacer is fitted. I think that a uniformly dark-coloured piece of antler looks rather uninteresting but can be improved considerably by sanding down lightly to give a nice mottled finish. The tips of the tines

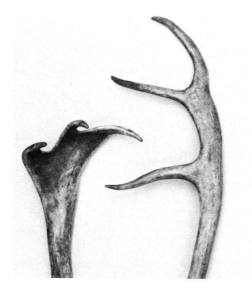

Reindeer antler, smooth like bone and randomly shaped.

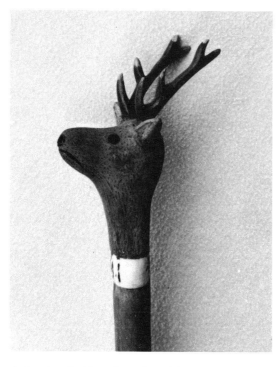

A deer head with antlers, shaped from reindeer antler.

also benefit from light sanding as this lightens their colour which looks particularly good on dark antler. You will often find that antler is encrusted with peat, leaf mould, or soil, but a bath in soapy water and a scrub with a nail brush will bring it up to a pristine state. If you do not care for light-coloured antler, stain with permanganate or coffee to the desired shade. All antler benefits from an application of linseed oil on occasion.

Antler will often have an oval-shaped cross-section but this is not a problem if you have a good selection of shanks as you can always lay hands on a matching shaped one. However, if you can not do this, fit the handle to a shank of the same diameter as the narrow section of the oval and then bevel down the two overlapping sides to make a smooth fit. A handle thicker than that of the shank looks all right if it is not too large but never fit a handle that is thinner as this always looks wrong. A finger-grooved handle can be considerably thicker than the shank as the grooves lessen the bulky appearance.

Some dog owners like to have an antler handle with a built-in whistle. These are not too difficult to make and if you are very fortunate you may be able to fashion one that blows at your first attempt. Drill out a hole in the end of the tine of the walker handle – a 1in (2.5cm) depth will suffice. Cut out a notch in the top of the tine ¾in (2cm) from the end, with a vertical cut nearest the end and a sloping cut (45 degrees) beyond. This notch will need to penetrate into the drilled-out portion. Then push a piece of dowel longer than the drilled hole and of the same diameter, with just a thin sliver shaved off the length of it, into the hole with the flat surface uppermost. Now try to whistle. If it makes no sound, shave off a little more of the dowel and twist it slightly in the hole as a very slight change in position can make all the difference. Once you get a whistle note, mark the position of the dowel carefully, extract it, apply glue to the uncut portion and push home. The protruding end can then be trimmed off and the antler mouthpiece smoothed down.

You may come across sets of mounted antler in places like antique shops that can be bought at a low price but, as they are usually trophies, they are quite often too bulky to be of any great use for stick-making. However, you might be fortunate and get the chance of Indian Sambar stag which is rather similar in shape to red deer antler but much more solid with scarcely any pith and often more deeply grooved. It is used for handles mainly on good-quality cutlery. Some species of American deer too have good-quality antlers but these are rarely seen for sale.

8 Deer Foot Handles

Hairy handles have never appealed to me and they most certainly could never equal the pleasure in handling a comfortable wood or horn hand piece, even when they are dry; when wet, any attraction they possess at all diminishes rapidly. Despite this, they do seem to command a certain following among stickmakers.

The feet of red deer and fallow are normally too large for handles but those of roe are just right. If possible, obtain the rear feet as they are marginally bigger than the front ones and a more suitable size for the stickmaker. First, wash the feet thoroughly in soapy water then rinse and place as soon as possible in a bath of surgical spirit; ensuring that they are fully submerged. A plastic sweet jar makes an ideal container. They must be kept there for at least a week but can be left indefinitely until such time as they are required. The spirit will season the foot, preventing both deterioration and ensuring that the skin does not loosen nor the hair drop out later on. It also eliminates any smell which would otherwise linger (and be particularly noticeable if the handle became wet).

There are two basic styles of handle:
Thumb piece handle On removal from the spirit, wash the foot in soapy water then rinse out and dry for an hour or two.

Then part the toes and, with a sharp knife, craft tool or similar, cut down through the tendon joining them and remove any protruding cartilage, skin, etc. The tendon pulled in the toes together tightly making it impossible to hold comfortably as a thumb piece, but, once severed, the toes can be parted easily. Next, fashion a slightly curved saddle of horn, antler or hardwood of suitable shape and dimension to hold a thumb comfortably. Glue into place between the toes and loop a string over the toe ends to pull together slightly and prevent them from splaying out at too wide an angle. Lay out the foot on a piece of board with a nail or two on either side of the toes to hold the saddle firmly in place. Leave in position for two to three weeks in a warm place to allow it to set and to let any residual smell from the spirit disperse.

Right-angle handle Treat in the same way as the thumb piece initially but, on removal from the spirit, put the foot on the board in a right-angle position and place a few nails along the outer edges to hold it in position. Again, the foot should be set permanently within two to three weeks.

With both types of handle, the toe nails or hooves can be enhanced by applying a dab of black shoe polish then buffing up with a rag.

FIXING THE HANDLE TO THE SHANK

To fix the thumb piece, saw through the bone just above the first joint – the right-angle handle will need a further 3–4in (7.5–10cm). The bone is oval in shape and about ¾in (2cm) across the widest part. Obtain a ¾in (2cm) piece of copper brass pipe (plumbers always have offcuts) and cut off a ½in length. Hammer this over the end of the exposed bone but underneath the skin, which should be eased up slightly beforehand with a knife point. To secure this, tap in a small wedge on either side of the oval section of bone where not up against the pipe, or fill in the gap with a glue/horn dust mixture. Then drill up through the bone to accept a pin or dowel fixing. Before glueing up, fashion a collar an inch (2.5cm) or so in length to fit over the joint. Antler would be the most appropriate choice. The ½in (1.3cm) length of pipe around the bone will prevent any splitting which might occur with the lateral pressure of the pin or dowel when the stick is in use. Apart from being attractive, the collar also strengthens the joint.

Other examples of deer-foot handles have been devised – such as the one made by removing the skin from the foot leaving only the toes or hooves attached. After seasoning, this is stretched over an old wooden umbrella handle or something similar, of suitable dimensions, and sewn up using cobblers' waxed thread. The jointing is by pin or dowel through handle and shank. However, I feel that the end result does not really justify the time and effort involved and can not begin to compare – apart from the novelty value – with the trusty trinity of wood, antler and horn handles. Deer feet do have one advantage over antler – they cost nothing.

9 Horn

Staffs and crooks have long been associated with authority or leadership but have also had a functional use since earliest times among farming communities. No doubt the earliest ones in rural districts were of wood, but adding a head of ramshorn was a natural development in sheep rearing districts, although in some areas of southern England where the flocks are more docile than the hill sheep, leg crooks of iron are still in use. (As a matter of interest, full-size crooks made entirely of alloy, shank included, are sold at farm suppliers nowadays, and pretty awful they look too!) The home of stick dressing, which is the shaping and carving of both wood and horn handled sticks, is often stated to be in Northumberland and the Borders. This is nothing more than local chauvinism, however, as the stick dressers of Durham, Yorkshire, Cumbria, Lancashire, Derbyshire and Wales will no doubt testify.

RAM'S HORN

The strongest and best ram's horn for stickmaking comes from hill sheep; a lot of lowland breeds are hornless, anyway. Horn from Swaledale, Herdwick, Cheviot, Welsh Mountain, Derbyshire Lonk and Scottish Blackface is probably the most popular among stick dressers. For really ornate carving, the Dorset Horn – if it can be had – is favoured as it is considerably bulkier than most other breeds. Jacobs is seen more nowadays, reflecting both the demand there is for its beautiful, vari-coloured horn and the increasing popularity of the breed.

Up to the 1960s, good ram's horn was plentiful but today it is in very short supply due to the changes in farming practices. Rams are sent to the abattoir at a much earlier date than previously and the use of feeding concentrate results in softer horns. The young rams produce

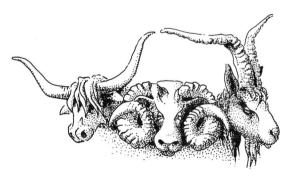

Highland cow, ram and billy-goat horn all make good handles.

48

fine looking horns but they consist mainly of the growing core or gowk with just a thin horn covering. An older ram will have perhaps similarly sized horns but they will be much more solid with less core. A really good horn would be 14–16in (0.4–0.5m) measured along the outer edge, and would have little or even no core evident at the base. A reasonable horn of the same length would have a core of up to three-quarters of the diameter of the base with a minimum thickness of horn all around the rim of ¼in (0.6cm). A poor horn would be nearly all core at the base with just a thin skin of horn of ⅛in (0.3cm) or less. One of the problems in stickmaking is preventing this white core from showing through. After a few weeks, the core will usually loosen inside the horn and can be removed by rapping the horn against a kerb or the edge of a work-bench. The depth of the hollow part remaining can then be measured and this will indicate the actual amount of solid horn. All horn needs at least a year to season after leaving the animal; if used before this it is liable to creep back out of shape after the handle has been made.

Ram's horn is usually not too difficult a horn to work with. It is not very closely grained and does not take an unduly long time to heat up to the malleable stage. (Jacobs horn is more easily worked than other breeds, being rather softer.) It does not crack easily under pressure and will not change colour when heated, unless actually singed. The usual colour varies from a pale straw to a deep honey shade, interspersed in the case of Blackface with random black lines running longitudinally. Jacobs is creamy coloured to white with clouded portions of deep-brown to

Ram's horn: (left to right) poor; reasonable; good.

black. Any ram's horn can be coloured in parts by a pink or reddish tinge, caused by blood diffusion usually after the animal has been fighting. I feel this always lends to its attraction, although some stick show judges would not agree. The natural horn is rough and will have a concave side, sometimes quite pronounced. This is usually called the bad side, because the horn is often quite deeply 'fingerprinted' and has occasional fissures cutting across its length. In some horn, the last few inches towards the tip, apart from being concave, will also be extremely thin and this type is not well liked by stick dressers. The flat section will usually have to be cut off and only on odd occasions can it be incorporated as the tail of a leaping trout.

Unfortunately, it is usually impossible to spot faults in the horn in its rough state, as any that are there have been crusted over with growing horn and often only come to light after work on a handle has commenced. The commonest is probably a blood clot or blister, usually caused when the animal has been fighting or after an ingrowing horn has been heated to bend away from the head. On occasion, a deep fissure or crack will be found, usually filled with dirt, fortunately this can often be discovered before the horn is worked.

For a full-size crook you will need a horn 14–16in (40–50cm) long; for a market stick (nose-in) or a smaller crook type, 10–12in (25–30cm) will suffice. A leg crook needs the same length as a full crook because, although it is narrow across the crown, it has a long nose, with neck to match. Another common stick is the half-head, which has a normal neck and crown but no nose – in other words, only one bend. A bird or animal head (badger, pheasant, etc.) is carved as an integral part of the crown, so a decent thickness of horn is required there and this is a popular use for a horn that has a very flat tip that will require removal.

COW HORN

This is probably the most beautiful of all horn, ranging from white and cream to olive, brown, deep-red and black shades. To these can be added the characteristic green hue caused by the sulphur released when the horn is heated and put under pressure. Cow horn appears to be the only horn to contain sulphur as this colour never appears in other kinds. The main drawback in working with cow horn is the extreme difficulty experienced in obtaining good horn. There are few horned cattle left in Great Britain as the majority are de-horned at an early age. The one most likely to be met with is the Highland breed, which has probably the most beautiful of all horn and this can be in excess of 30in (75cm) long. Another possibility is Jersey or Ayrshire but neither are met, wearing their horns, with regularity nowadays. I have obtained various cow horns from the local vet.

The big problem with all cow horn is that it is mainly hollow along the greater part of its length, a 30in (76cm) Highland horn, for instance, may only have three or four inches (7.5–10cm) of solid at the tip. This makes for a lot of work squeezing up and a success rate in making stick handles of perhaps only one in three. This is assuming a mainly hollow horn is being used; if you manage to obtain one with a fair proportion of solid in it, then cow horn is not any more difficult to work with than ram's horn. It is essential, however, that no attempt is made to speed up the heating process, prior to squeezing up, by letting the heat source play into the hollow portion of the horn, as this will inevitably lead to delamination. The onion skin effect will also occur if attempts are made to remove the outer layer of horn prior to heating or if a groove is made in the horn to help the bending process.

As the first bend for the heel of the handle will be at a hollow part of the horn, some method has to be devised of stopping the horn from folding in on itself at this point. As good a plan as any is to reinsert the original core as a tailor-made plug which will inhibit the internal distortion as the horn bends. Another method I have used with success is to pack the hollow horn with sand and plug the end to prevent spillage. The actual bending should also be done very slowly. Similarly, when initially squeezing up the base to bring it down to reasonable dimensions, it is advisable to leave the core in place or to insert a tapering wood plug – either will be partly forced out under pressure but will prevent the horn buckling. After a handle has been shaped, there will always be a hollow section remaining at the base and this should be filled using a mixture of glue and horn dust or filings; after setting, joint in the usual way.

One peculiarity of cow horn is that the cow produces the best horn for stickmaking; the bull may have larger horns but they are very thin shelled. It is possible to obtain imported ox horn from Africa and India but I have yet to see any that is of stickmaking quality, though sometimes of impressive size it is invariably hollow, thin shelled and delaminates very easily. Rare breeds and safari parks could possibly be a source of supply as they are trying to resuscitate some of the Longhorn types.

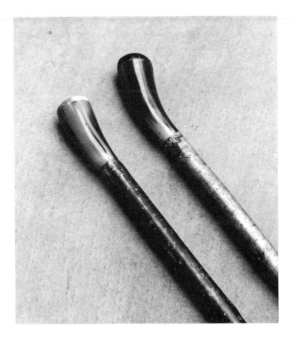

Cow horn. These mainly hollow pieces have been plugged and horn capped to make attractive handles.

BILLY-GOAT HORN

This is another horn which is not too easy to come by as most domestic animals are hornless breeds but, in the north at least, the Old English type, complete with horns, is still fairly popular. There are also scattered around Great Britain various herds of wild goats, although it is inaccurate to so describe them as they are really feral, having been released or escaped from domestic stock originally. The current estimate of their numbers is upwards of 10,000 so they are by no means rare.

The wild billy produces horns similar to the domestic strain, although obviously the size reflects the health of the animal and the available food supply. There are two distinct horn shapes. In the first, the horns sweep back from the head in a crescent, in the second they curve back for about half of their length then twist out sideways. As with cow horn, a large proportion of horns are predominately hollow with only the 3–4in (around 9cm) towards the tip being solid. A good billy-goat horn would be about 30in (76cm) in length with a quarter of that solid and the rim of the hollow base, when the horn is cut to a 15in (38cm) length, being at least ¼in (0.6cm) thick. The outer curve of the horn always has a distinctive humped ridge along its length and this will need to be removed before work starts on the handle.

The cross-section of the horn is a rather flattened oval and of course this will require rounding up for stickmaking. The procedure is similar to that used with cow horn, with the hollow section being plugged either with the original core or packed with sand, but most of the squeezing up will obviously be required on the end walls of the oval section. The horn has a satin-like grain and when polished will vary in colour depending on the animal it came from: a black or dark-grey billy will produce black horn when polished but usually this will have a faint, underlying brownish mottle which is rather nice; vari-coloured animals will have horn that ranges from olive to buff with rich tones of red and brown. It is similar to cow's horn for bending and shaping once the original oval section has been reworked.

There is one other point which must be made about goat horn: it is rather strong smelling. All horn smells when heated and I do not find it unpleasant, but goat horn is in a class of its own in this respect. It has been described as being worse than that of a flatulent ferret, so you have been warned! Wear old clothes and a hat as the smell lingers.

BUFFALO HORN

Two kinds of buffalo horn are used in stickmaking: African, which is jet black and takes a very high gloss, and Indian or Burmese, usually known as green or coloured, which ranges from grey and olive, sometimes with green or blue tints, through to reddish brown.

Black Buffalo

This is jet black with a high gloss and may contain lighter-coloured mottle, particularly near the core. It is probably the hardest horn there is, being very dense in the grain and consequently heavy. It is therefore much harder to work than ram's horn. It is becoming increasingly popular, owing to the shortage of ram's horn. The hollow portion of this horn is cut off before being sold and so what you buy is solid horn and a typical horn bought for stickmaking would be oval in section and from 15–18in (38–46cm) long, with a diameter at the base of roughly 3in (7.5cm) by 1½in (3.8cm). This would be from 1 to 1½lb (0.5–0.7kg) in weight. Because of the very close grain it heats very slowly and, as with any kind of horn, any singed patches that appear in the process must be removed immediately before they spread and also prevent the heat from penetrating the horn uniformly. To determine whether the horn has heated up sufficiently to be workable, put one end in a vice and pull sideways – if the horn can be moved by hand it is ready. Do not attempt the first bend in one stage but do it gradually in three or four stages to prevent internal stress fractures which would appear later. Before shaping the first bend, use a round rasp to make a groove on each side of the horn at the spot to be bent.

Coloured Buffalo

Coloured buffalo is much softer than the black variety and consequently that much easier to work. It is about the same consistency as ram's horn. It ranges from pale grey, through green tinges to reddish brown. Unfortunately, it is now much harder to obtain as most of the horn imported is used in button making. The basic dimensions are similar to the black horn and some very nice handles indeed have been turned out using this horn. Occasionally, the cross-section is rather flat in shape but this is easily remedied simply by heating and compressing in a vice to thicken up the shape of the base.

It cannot be stressed too strongly that horn will only move and shape successfully when it is ready, and this state is determined by testing in a vice – if it moves fairly easily by hand then you have reached that stage. Always heat horn on either side of the part requiring bending – 4in (10cm) or so overall is about right – and before heating brush engine oil over the area. This heats up to a high temperature, spreads the heat more easily and, most important of all, replenishes any natural oil in the horn forced out in the heating process.

OXHORN (IMPORTED)

This is traditionally black, shading to white and cream in parts. It often has a red-brown tinge. It is rarely good enough for stickmaking.

10 Plain Horn Handles

Given a good ram's horn, and by that I mean one that is at least 10–12in (25–30cm) long, with little or none of that consisting of core (or hollow), it is possible to make a horn handle (or 'horn heid' in the north) without any special apparatus apart from a vice or even just a sash cramp. The result will be the common umbrella handle shape and no doubt this rather simplistic style is the very first one that many stickmakers accomplish. However, having got over the first hurdle, and with appetites whetted by the displays at stick shows, they will be keen to improve their knowledge of the craft.

There are as many ways of bending and shaping horn as there are spines on a blackthorn and some very esoteric devices have been dreamt up to achieve the goal. If you are not fortunate enough to live in the North-East or in the Borders where night classes in the craft are commonplace, you would be well advised to seek the help of a horn head maker who does not mind imparting his knowledge. It is most decidedly a craft where an ounce of demonstration is worth a ton of explanation. If you wish to succeed with ram's horn, do not settle for a display using buffalo horn as this requires a different technique entirely.

RAM'S HORN

In cross-section, ram's horn is crudely triangular at the base with rounded corners as a rule. One side is invariably concave along it's length, sometimes quite prominently, with a pronounced overhang at the top. The other sides are normally convex but the horn may be deeply fisssured across its length and marked with prominent 'fingerprints' usually on the concave face. It is a moot point as to whether a beginner should start with a good horn or a poor one, assuming that he has a choice. A good horn could possibly be ruined through inexperience, although this can be avoided by proceeding cautiously, but a poor one can present so many problems that the novice might despair of ever learning the craft. Leonard Parkin, who after thirty years as a professional horn craftsman was arguably the most skilled exponent of the 'horn heid' in the country, used to say, 'Anybody can make a handle out of a good horn, but it takes something else to make one from a poor one.'

The essence of working with horn is to utilize, as far as possible, the complete bulk of the horn that is available. By that I mean that hollow portions at the base of the horn, for instance, need not be discarded as is often recommended. The horn is reworked in a fashion that entirely changes its original shape but in doing so as little as possible is removed.

Apparatus and Tools

Before starting, you will require the following:

1. A bottle jack. Any pressure from 2 tons (2,000kg) upwards is acceptable.
2. A frame 18in (46cm) high and 1ft sq (30cm sq) from welded, 1in (2·5cm) thick angle iron. The frame should have a floor and roof made of ⅜in

(1cm) thick steel. A loose centre plate, 10in sq (25cm sq), is also required, either in ¾in (1·94cm) thick steel or in 1in (2·5cm) thick hardwood (oak or elm is ideal). This apparatus is for straightening the sideways curl and flattening any hollow portions of the horn after softening.

3. A bench or engineer's vice. Drill a hole, ⅜in (1cm) in diameter and ¾in (1·9cm) deep in the centre of the flat bed of the vice, ¾in (1·9cm) in front of the front jaw.
4. A round metal cylinder (a dolly), 6in (15cm) long and 1½in (3·8cm) in diameter with a bevelled neck ½in (1·3cm) from one end. The neck is ⅛in (0·3cm) deep in the centre and 1in (2·5cm) wide. Drill a hole, ⅜in (1cm) in diameter and ¾in (1·9cm) deep, in the centre of the dolly at each end.

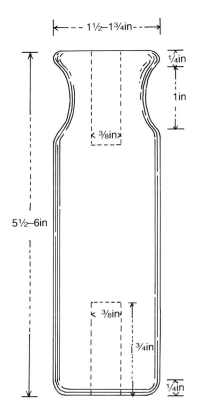

A dolly for horn working.

Metal and hardwood clamps for squeezing up horn.

5. A 1½ × ⅜in (3·8 × 1cm) bolt, with the head cut off, or a similar length of appropriate studding. This drops into the hole drilled in the bed of the vice and the dolly drops over the protruding portion. The dolly will stand up from the vice jaws by two to three inches (5–7·5cm).

6. A steel plate ½in (1·3cm) thick and 6in sq (15cm sq) with a 3in sq (7·5cm sq) piece cut out of one corner. This is to be affixed to the front of the rear jaw of the vice with the cut-out corner uppermost. There are usually two retaining screws in vice jaws and these can be replaced with slightly longer ones to allow for the thickness of the plate.

7. A sash cramp – 15–18in (27·5–45cm).

8. A large saucepan or similar for boiling horn.

9. A blowlamp or hot-air gun/paint stripper.

10. Hardwood formers 1in (2·5cm) thick. These are taken from the inside shapes of a crook, a market stick (nose-in) and a leg crook. Try to borrow or obtain a good model in each case from which to construct the former.

11. Several pairs of clamps made of 3–4in (7·5–10cm) lengths of steel or alloy pipe cut lengthways and with welded stays on the back to prevent pipes from splaying out. The internal diameters should be in sizes between 2in and 1¼in (5–3·2cm). These could be replaced by hardwood blocks drilled and sawn lengthways with the grain.

12. Sundries: a waterspray bottle; rasps; engine oil and brush; various wood or rubber wedges; a wood peg tapering from ¾in (1·9cm) down to ¼in (0.6cm).

Method

Simmer horn in a pan of boiling water for twenty minutes to half an hour. Test for readiness by placing 2–3in (5–7·5cm) of the tip of the horn in the vice and pulling backwards. If the horn is ready, it will give easily. Place the horn on top of the loose plate on the jack in the flattening frame and wind up, ensuring that the horn does not ride off sideways. Check that the curl on the horn has been pulled into line with the rest and that any hollow portion towards the base has been flattened. Leave it to set for about half an hour. You should now have a flattish, horseshoe shaped piece of horn, at least ½in (1·3cm) thick and 2in (5cm) or more wide at the base.

The first stage in shaping is to form the heel which is the first main bend in the horn where the crown comes away at an angle from the neck. This is usually at a point between 3–4in (7·5–10cm) up from the base. Before any horn is bent, it must be heated but it is no good heating solely at the point where the bending is to take place. Heat at least 2in (5cm) on either side to allow for the horn to stretch, otherwise splitting will occur. It is advisable to brush engine oil (not from the sump or you will produce a smelly, smoky atmosphere!) around the part of the horn to be heated. Never play your heat source, whether naked flame or hot air, in one place for longer than a few seconds; rather move it back and forth along the 4in (10cm) or so to be heated, turning the horn regularly to ensure even distribution. Renew the oil as necessary and, if any parts of the horn do become scorched, rasp or sand off that portion immediately as not only will it spread if left but it will also act as a barrier to prevent the heat penetrating further. The heating will probably take up to twenty minutes. Test in the vice by pulling against the heated portion – if it moves without having to pull too hard, it is ready.

Now place the horn horizontally in the vice with the shaped neck of the dolly against the inside curve of the horn, 1in (2·5cm) beyond where the heel is required. The dolly will act in conjunction with the steel backing plate as a vertical rolling pin in shaping up the softened horn. The uppermost part of the horn should be the 'bad' side, i.e. the side which was originally concave and usually more heavily marked with fissures and 'fingerprint' indentations than the other. Although now flattened, this side will no doubt still be rather lumpy and with a trace of overhang along the outer curve and it is advisable to smooth this down somewhat before shaping.

The other side of the horn, the 'good' side, does not require any action to be taken on it during the general shaping process as it rounds out naturally under pressure from the dolly, having been that shape (convex) originally. Wind in the vice and the flattened horn should round out with the pressure. Hold the dolly in that position for a few seconds then unwind, slide the horn back along towards the base only as far as the next part to be reshaped, about ½in (1·3cm), then wind the vice up again and this next section should bulge out to add to the original part. Continue for another one or two squeeze-ups only, holding the pressure on for a few seconds in each case. Speed is of the essence at this stage; you should manage three to four squeezes before reheating is required.

If at any stage the horn does not round

outwards, reposition the horn in the vice so that the neck of the dolly is putting pressure on at a slightly different angle. The heel should now just about be shaped, with the crown coming away from the neck of the horn (which remains flat) approximately at the correct angle, with the squeezed-up part round in shape. Now heat up the neck down to the base of the horn, after removing any uneven or rough bulges that remain after the flattening process.

When ready, place this part in the largest of your clamps – the 2in (5cm) one – and squeeze up in the vice with the base of the horn uppermost. Although flattened, you will see that the original hollow part has not entirely disappeared and, before exerting any great pressure on to it, tap the tapering wood peg into the centre of the hollow part. Should you be fortunate enough to be dealing with a horn that does not have any hollow part (this will be extremely unlikely) the peg will not be required. The function of the peg is to prevent the hollow part from distorting internally once the rounding out process with the clamping commences. Once you have wound in the clamps as far as they will go, leave to set. The cooling process can be speeded up by spraying with cold water. There will almost certainly be two raised rims of horn which have squeezed out between the clamps and these should be rasped or sanded off before re-heating.

Step down to the second largest set of clamps and, after heating, squeeze up again, tapping in the peg as before, and repeat in sequence with the other clamps down to the second smallest. It is not always necessary to re-heat at each stage because sometimes the clamps come together fairly easily and not much heat has been lost so the next set of clamps can be applied with very little delay.

With one stage still to go, you will almost certainly notice that the hole in the horn is off-centre despite the use of the peg during clamping. It is now advisable to centre up this hole by enlarging with a ½in (1·3cm) or a ⅝in (1·6cm) drill. After the final clamping, the side walls of the horn will probably now be from ¼–½in (0·6–1·3cm) thick. If the hole is still too far off-centre, plug with a glue and horn dust or filings mix. The handle is now beginning to shape up with the neck and the beginning of the crown in the round.

Now go back to using the dolly, starting at the crown next to where you heated and shaped up initially, ensuring that any lumpy parts or overhang have been removed prior to heating. Work your way in stages along the crown towards the nose. The horn will be tapering along this length and should not take as long to heat up but will require careful positioning of the dolly to ensure that the essential rounding out occurs. As the horn is not so thick, it is advisable at times to sand or

Horn being shaped with a dolly against a back plate in a vice. (The corner piece of the back plate can be cut away to facilitate positioning of the horn.)

rasp a flat surface on to the inside curve to give the dolly better purchase, but do not remove too much horn as the white may be near to the surface. The horn thins out towards the nose and may also tend to fold over on itself under pressure. At the first sign of this, take off the pressure and try repositioning the horn in relation to the dolly. This is where the cut-out section of the backing plate can come into its own, as the horn can be placed in the reverse direction with the dolly bearing down on the outer edge of the horn instead of the inner. If by chance you do end up with a folded-over portion of horn, take it off with a rasp or sander as you will not be able to straighten it out again. This is where there is a danger of the white coming through. You should be able to round up to the nose but, if there is still 1 or 2in (2·5 or 5cm) that remains obstinately flat towards the tip, it might be possible to cut this off, depending on the overall length of horn available for the nose.

Alternatively, you can consider a change in style of the handle, as a nose-in market stick is about 2in (5cm) shorter than a crook. And a nicely proportioned market stick would be a far better proposition than a crook with a flat or insignificant tip to the nose which would upset the overall balance of the handle.

Nose In or Nose Out?

We have now reached the stage of shaping the horn around the wood former. You will probably find that the former cannot be pushed into position as the handle mouth is probably too narrow. Heat the horn along the crown and overlap on to the nose. When ready, insert the nose-in style former into position and

Ram's horn: (left to right) natural; flattened; shaped into a handle.

place the horn in the vice with the neck and nose being between the jaws. Do not tighten up the vice but just use sufficient pressure to hold the horn in place. Put the sash cramp at right angles to the vice, gripping the base of the former and the crown of the horn, having first placed one of the smaller of the clamps lengthways over the crown to prevent the sash cramp jaw from flattening the horn. Wind in the sash cramp which will pull down the crown on to the former. Allow to set.

If you wish to retain the nose-in style, all that remains is to decide on the length and final angle of the nose, before finishing, re-heating and pulling in the nose further to the former, between the vice, if that is the angle desired. If a crook shape has been decided on, heat up the final 4in (10cm) of the horn and, when ready, put the crook shape former in place with the dolly opposite the portion that curves out near the end of the nose. The gentle pressure of the dolly will press the

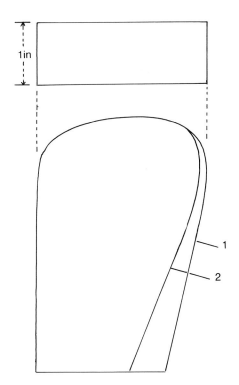

A template for a hardwood former of the nose-in market stick style.

59

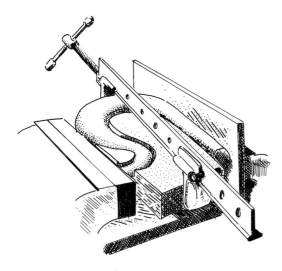

A droopy nose being corrected with a sash cramp pushing up the former into the crown of the handle.

horn into the curve of the former and the nose will come out in the crook position. Use the plain cylinder end of the dolly as the neck part would flatten the nose unduly. The tip of the nose will occasionally lean sideways at this stage and should be pulled back into place with a pair of flat grips until set.

Finally, take the horn out of the vice, remove the former, and look at the whole handle, both head-on and in profile, to see if there are any divergencies from the correct line. Two common faults found at this stage would be a droopy nose, which is when the front part of the crown as it meets the nose is lower than the angle of the heel, and a nose slightly out of line in relation to the vertical neck, when looked

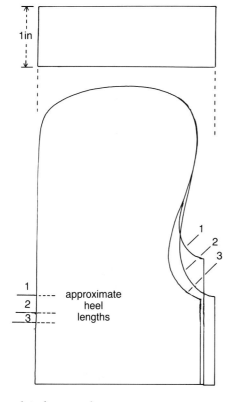

A template for a crook.

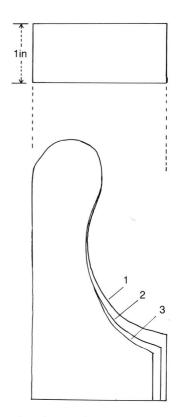

A template for a leg crook.

at from the front. The droopy nose can be corrected by heating the front part of the crown, replacing the former and, with the sash cramp, pushing the former up into the crown until the correct set is obtained. The nose out of line is easily straightened by heating and pushing into position with a wedge but careful monitoring is essential.

When deciding on the final shape of the tip, it is better not to saw off any surplus horn as this will expose the white. Heat and try to shear off with a series of nips using a pair of pliers. This should round the edges of the horn over any exposed white and thus hide it. Alternatively, experiment with the bit of a soldering iron, either manual or electric, which when heated will melt the horn which is then pressed over any exposed white, but care must be taken to prevent scorching. Once satisfied as to the final overall shape, dress down with emery in successively finer grades, paying particular attention to any wrinkling on the inside curves.

Leg Crook

The leg crook is undertaken in the same way as above but the following two points should be watched:

The neck of a leg crook should be longer than the market stick/crook style to compensate for the elongated nose. One regularly sees at shows leg crooks where the nose falls below the level of the joint between handle and shank, thus breaking one of the unwritten laws of stickmaking. There will normally be sufficient horn to allow for a long neck as the crown is short.

As the horn is virtually doubling back on itself in a comparatively small radius along the crown, particular care must be

taken in heating the horn. If necessary, do the bend in two stages rather than risk splitting the horn.

Ram's Curl

The ram's curl is identical to the market stick/crook style for two-thirds of its length, along the neck and the crown, but has an extra 3–4in (7·5–10cm) of horn which completes the curl. It is a useful type to try if the last few inches of the nose are 'rat-tailed', having a narrow taper which would otherwise upset the balance of a good neck and crown. To shape the curl, heat the nose portion from the end of

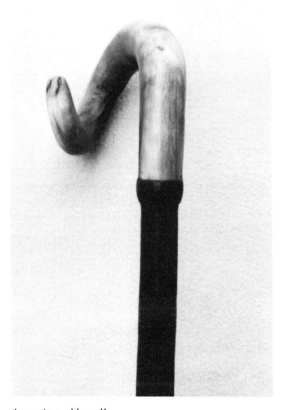

A ram's curl handle.

the crown and, holding either the dolly or a suitable piece of rounded wood horizontally under the crown, bend the horn underneath in a loop away from the line of the crown, and for the last 2in (5cm) or so swing the tip out slightly further. If the horn is long enough, it is sometimes possible to 'loop the loop' or virtually have a double curl. Bear in mind that there must be sufficient clearance for the fingers to grip the handle with this style and place the curl accordingly. Do not let the bottom of the curl fall below the line of the joint. This handle is much easier to shape if the curl naturally follows the outward shape of the horn before flattening, i.e. with either a left- or right-handed bias. The curl can be held in place by hand until set. Holding a damp cloth over the horn will speed up the process.

BUFFALO HORN

Black buffalo and coloured buffalo are worked in the same way, except that coloured buffalo, being a softer horn, requires less heating. The apparatus for bending is simple: a sash cramp and a wood former. The former is made from hardwood, cut lengthways with the grain, 12in (30cm) × 4in (10cm) × 1½in (3·8cm) thick. Cut a crescent-shaped section out of one side (centred up) 7in (17·5cm) wide and 2½in (6·3cm) deep. Groove the ends of the crescent slightly with a round rasp to create shallow hollows running for 2in (5cm) from the rim of the crescent down into the recess. These will hold the horn more firmly in position eventually and inhibit side-slip.

Brush with oil and heat the horn after cutting a shallow groove with a round rasp on either side of the inside curve where you want the first main bend at the heel to be, normally 4–5in (10–12·5cm) up from the base. Do not remove any surplus horn as yet, although it is probably 2–3in (5–7·5cm) in diameter at the base. The heating will take approximately three-quarters of an hour for black buffalo but only about half that time for coloured as it is a softer horn. As with all horn, heat at least a 4–5in (10–12·5cm) area around where the bend is to be, removing any scorch marks as they appear and renewing the oil as necessary. When ready, lay across the former on the cut-out crescent portion with the spot to be bent half-way across and put the sash cramp with the movable jaw on the horn and the wind up part on the back of the former. Slide up one of the smaller metal clamps used for squeezing between the cramp jaw and the horn to stop the cramp riding off the horn. Wind up with the pressure on the part to be bent and once this part meets with the base of the crescent you will find that you have close to a right-angle bend in the horn. Leave to set.

If you have reached the correct temperature with the heating up, the horn should bend readily but wind up slowly; if there is any resistance or indication of cracking, release pressure immediately. Remove any cracks that do appear to prevent any danger of enlargement. The second bend can be made by placing the heated, roughly L-shaped horn in the vice – after first grooving in the same way as before where the bend is to be. It is also advisable to slide two pieces of very coarse emery back to back between the end of the nose of the horn and the vice jaw to prevent slip Again, wind up slowly and watch for cracking. The final shaping is done between the normal market stick/ crook formers.

Buffalo horn being shaped with a sash cramp and a hardwood former.

COW HORN

Cow horn is shaped in the same way as the buffalo horn and utilizes the same former, but do *not* make any grooves in the horn where the bends are to be, and do not remove any surplus horn before heating either.

BILLY-GOAT HORN

Billy-goat horn is also worked in the same way as buffalo. This horn often has a tendency to be 'rat-tailed' towards the tip and lends itself to the ram's curl style of handle.

All horn is finished in the same way, using successive grades of emery down to 'wet and dry' paper (400 to 600 grit), followed by a final polish with either car rubbing compound or liquid metal cleaner. You should *not* varnish but you can use a little linseed oil when oiling the shank. When jointing, do not spoil the effect by using a metal collar – horn or antler is best.

If you have a large buffalo horn it is possible to make a horn handle from a piece cut from the base. This is simply cut out from a block of solid horn which needs to be 5in (12·5cm) long and at least 3 × 1in (7·5 × 2·5cm). The neck is fashioned parallel to the cut edge of the base and the

63

Three styles of handle that can be made from a block of solid buffalo horn.

crown from the length, with a nose-in style usually possible. As the neck is short it can be improved by the addition of a collar or spacer of antler cut proud and buffed down to the white. This is hardly stick dressing but it does, none the less, result in quite a presentable horn handle with a minimum of effort.

Similarly, a thumb stick handle can be fashioned from a block of horn. For this you need a horn piece about 3 × 2 × 1in (7·5 × 5 × 2·5cm). Portion out the horn so that approximately half of the length will be neck and the other half will provide the arms of the fork. First, drill a hole of at least ½in (1·3cm) width through the centre of the horn, 1½in (3·8cm) down from one end. Then saw down twice from the nearest end of the horn to the outer edge of the hole in each case. You will now have a ½in (1·3cm) wide and roughly 1½in (3·8cm) long U-shaped aperture let into one end of the horn. If the available width of the horn is nearer 3in (7·5cm) than 2in (5cm), a wider hole of up to 1in (2·5cm) could be drilled initially. Bevel off all cut edges of the aperture, particularly at the rounded base of the U shape.

After oiling, heat up the horn until workable then slowly hammer a wooden

A Rio rosewood crook and an Amazon rosewood market stick by Alan Thompson.

An elm burr leg crook by Frank Day.

A fancy wood crook by Fred Prickett.

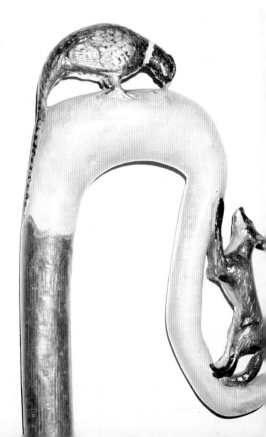

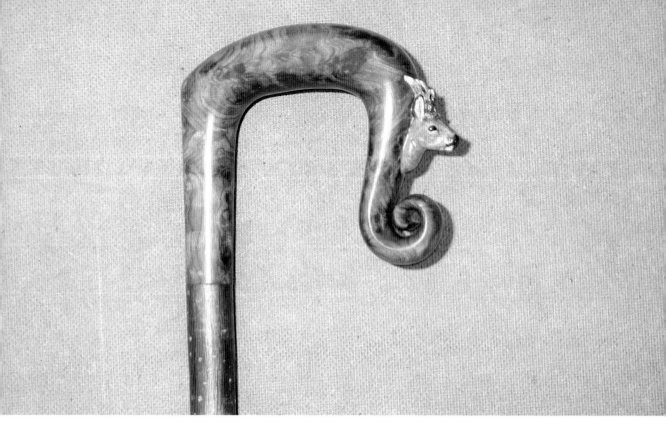

An elm burr fancy crook with a roe deer head by Frank Day.

A hazel crook by Frank Day.

A wood horse head by Alan Thompson.

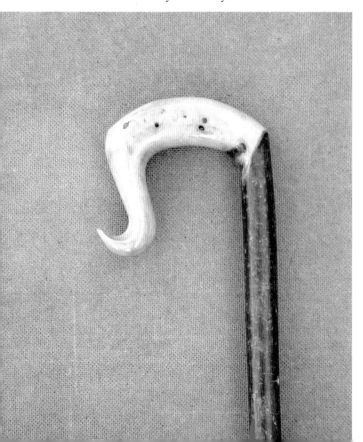

Antler thumbsticks: (left to right) red; fallow; roe.

Antler coronets. The darker coloured one has a wren farthing insert.

Ram's horn and coloured buffalo market sticks.

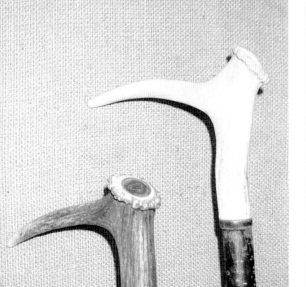

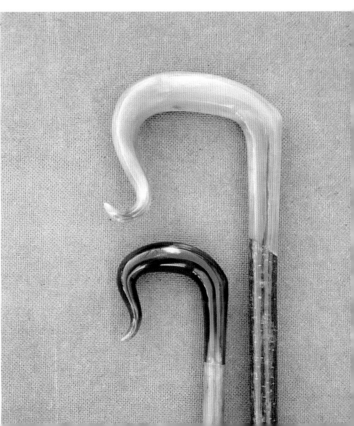

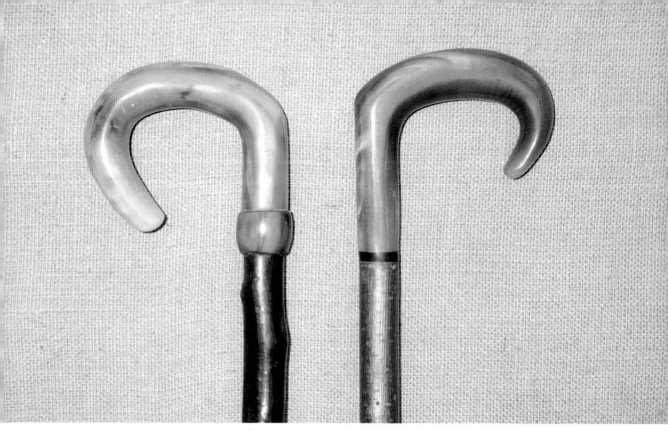

Coloured buffalo and ram's horn market sticks.

A collie on a ram's horn crook and a black
cock in buffalo by Frank Day.

Acorn and oak leaves on a ram's horn crook
by Frank Day.

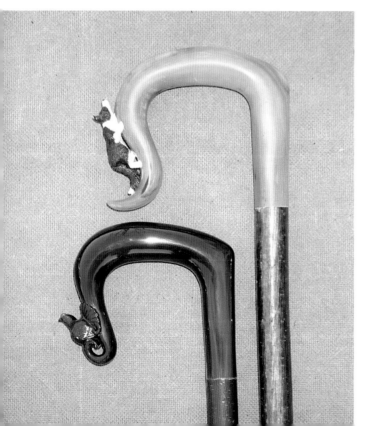

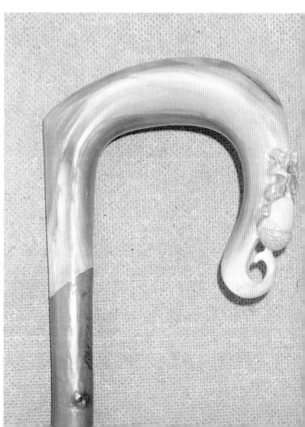

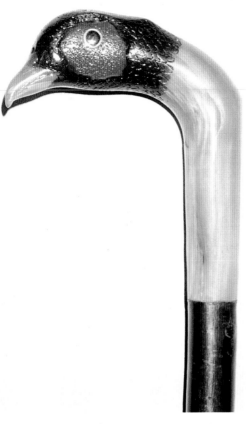

A pheasant half head by Leonard Parkin.

Highland Cow is probably the most beautiful of all horn.

A fox in black buffalo by Bill Canning.

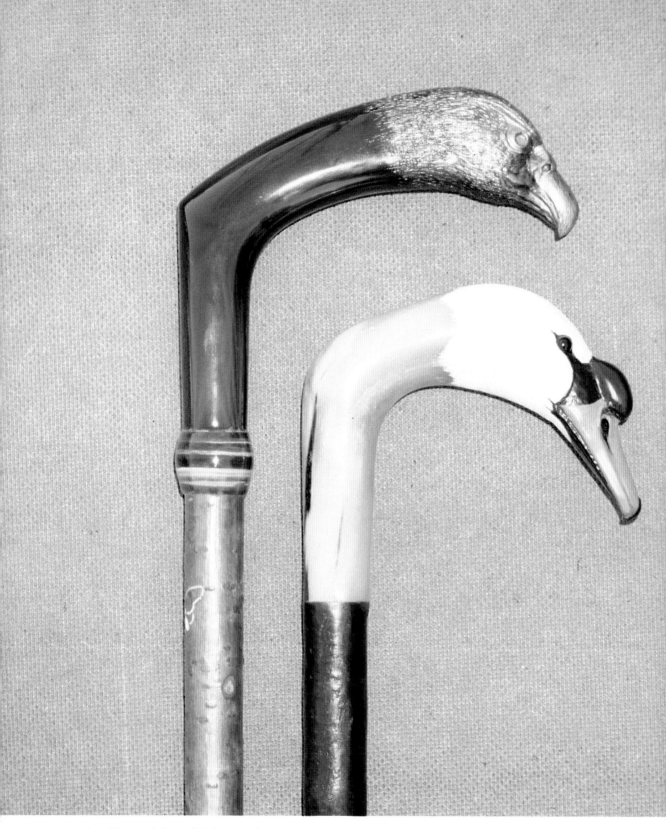

A golden eagle in buffalo horn and a ram's
horn swan by Frank Day.

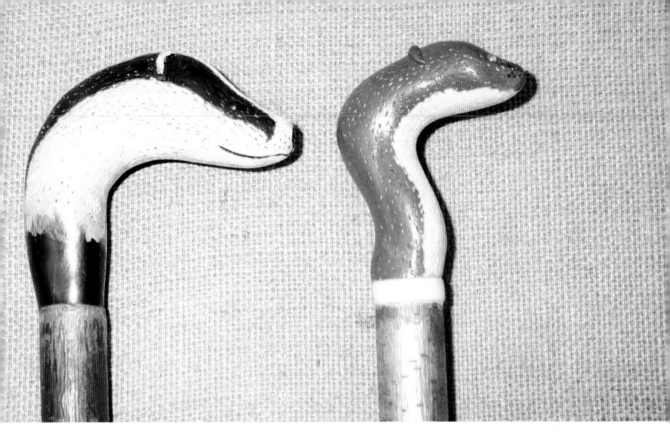

A badger in black buffalo horn and a weasel in reindeer antler.

An otter in buffalo horn by Alan Thompson.

An otter thumb piece in black buffalo by Alan Thompson.

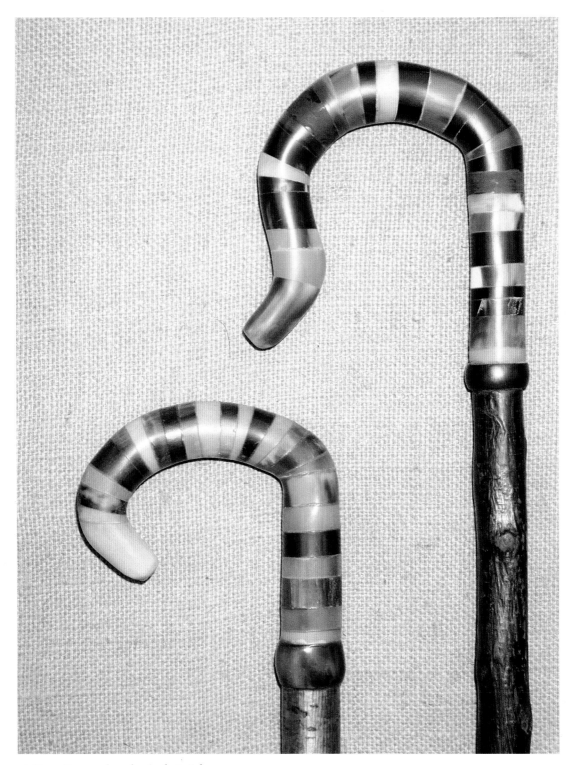

A Horn disc crook and a market stick.

peg (a piece of offcut shank is ideal) horizontally down into the U aperture. The diameter of this peg should be roughly ¼in (0·6cm) wider than the aperture width. This will widen the aperture by pushing the arms further apart. When set, remove the wooden peg, reheat the horn and repeat the process with a further peg, again ¼in (0·6cm) wider. This should result in a 1in (2·5cm) wide aperture which is adequate for most thumb pieces. You might find that the arms are splaying out too much in which case they can be pulled in slightly by gentle use of the sash cramp or a G-cramp. After removing the peg, shape the arms with a slight outward curve to the top with each arm eventually being a long, shallow S shape. Round out any flattish areas as required and bevel down the front base of the handle where the thumb will rest. Joint, then trim down the neck to fit as usual.

TUFNOL

This is actually a man-made material produced from compressed linen bound in glue but it has virtually the same look, feel and weight as horn (though it has a rather grain-like texture.) It is just about the most expensive stickmaking material there is but it does have the great advantage that it can be cut to shape simply from a board, and it makes a very hard-wearing stick handle indeed. Its main function is in the making of electrical circuit boards in industry and it is not easily obtainable in boards thicker than ½in (1·3cm). Fortunately, I was given some by a friend which was 1¼in (3·2cm) thick – ideal for stickmaking. It comes in different shades and I have seen handles in a mid-brown which I did not particularly care for, but the piece I received was a warm buff shade not unlike ram's horn.

First, draw the handle shape in outline on the material. If you have access to a band-saw you can cut this out easily enough but it is advisable to wear a mask as the dust can be very irritating. Alternatively, use a carpenters' bow-saw or a coping saw. Ensure that you cut wide of the outline throughout to allow for rounding off. Shaping can then be done using a powerfile or by rasping to a rough shape. Finish off with strapping and emery in the normal way.

You will find that the material is tough but workable and will not crack or flake in any way. It polishes up easily enough too (I use linseed oil) but a metal-cleaning liquid or a car-rubbing compound will bring up a good gloss.

11 Fancy Horn Handles

A handle can be fancy, i.e. decorated and/or carved, yet still be practical. Many stickmakers forget this and produce ornately carved and coloured sticks which are only good for hall stands or decoration – aptly described in the North as 'wall sticks'. What was a simple country craft has now been elevated to a higher art form but one which has, in many instances, lost the essential qualities of balance and proportion. Objects carved as appendages to the handle, whether birds, insects, animals or whatever, often impress as tributes to the observation, patience and skill of the maker but more often than not result in an impractical handle.

One of the few unwritten rules of horn stickmaking is that the whole handle must be made from one piece of horn, yet the common practice of inserting (usually) black buffalo horn eyes in a pheasant or trout carved in ram's horn is a common practice that is always accepted. A high proportion of fancy carved sticks have

A squirrel on the nose of a crook. A good subject with a graceful body and tail.

A collie on the nose of a crook. The head should be in line with the shoulders.

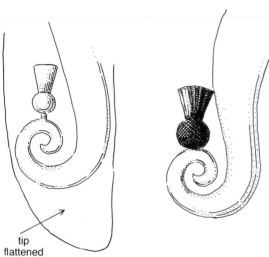

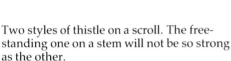
tip
flattened

Two styles of thistle on a scroll. The free-standing one on a stem will not be so strong as the other.

An alternative to the thistle design is the acorn with a pair of oak leaves on the crook nose.

had the carvings done on separate pieces of horn from that of the handle although it is almost impossible to detect the join as the carvings are normally coloured. Not that I think there is anything intrinsically wrong with this practice – if the two can be brought together to form one harmonious whole and the final result is a better stick then it is a case of the end justifying the means. By doing this, one can enjoy the best of both worlds: concentrating initially upon making a good shaped horn handle then transferring attention to doing likewise with the carving.

CROOK WITH SCROLL AND THISTLE

The traditional way to make this is to shape the neck and the crown in the usual way but to heat and flatten the last few inches of the nose. The design of the scroll and thistle is drawn on this flattened part and holes are drilled into both the centre of the scroll and usually at the back of the ball of the thistle. A coping saw is inserted through these holes and the back part of the thistle outline and the scroll itself is cut out. The finer shaping and finishing are done in a variety of ways using half-inch strapping to clean up the scroll, and knives, small rasps, needle files, etc. for work on the thistle. The initial flattening of the horn unfortunately often results in an insignifcant rat-tailed nose and a flat-tish, badly shaped or too small thistle. It is better by far to flatten the nose, in the first instance, only sufficiently to enable a decent scroll to be made, then make a good thistle from a separate piece of horn and glue and pin it to the scroll. If you are fortunate enough to have a good solid piece of horn towards the nose, then the thistle can be carved in one with the handle. Incidentally, the thistle should always be vertical and not lean in or out as is often seen.

67

CROOK WITH SCROLL AND ACORN

This is very similar to the thistle crook and is made in the same way. It is more appropriate than a thistle for an English-made stick and can be improved considerably by adding an oak leaf on the nose just behind the acorn. It can be relief carved if there is sufficient bulk of horn but this is seldom the case. However, it is a simple matter to carve a leaf from a piece of flat horn. Heat this for a minute or two with a hot-air gun to make it pliable, smear the back with glue and move into position on the nose. Tie with a few loops of cord to hold it in position until set. As with the thistle, the acorn should be vertical on the scroll.

LEAPING TROUT

This is a great favourite, probably because it fits comfortably in the hand, since it is, very crudely, an umbrella handle shape.

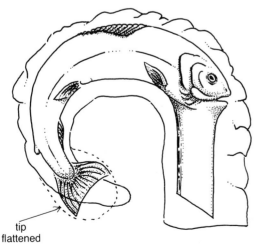

tip
flattened

The shaping of a trout from ram's horn.

Anyone who specializes in this type of stick will tell you that it is not essential to have a really good solid horn to make a decent handle. Often you will see examples where the head protrudes a good ½ – ¾in (1.3–1.9cm) from the neck of the horn, but again this is not absolutely necessary as I feel that the trout looks just as well with only ¼in (0.6cm) of head standing proud of the neck. The neck is usually short, 2in (5cm) being adequate up to the bottom of the jaw. Head and shoulders run smoothly to the midriff with little or no variation in diameter and the rear end tapers only marginally towards the tail. The usual practice for shaping the tail is to squeeze it up flat to get the width required, but this needs a reasonably thick horn tip initially. If there is not sufficient bulk of horn towards the tip I would suggest that the tail be fashioned from a separate piece of horn then jointed to the remainder neatly. The body is not round in shape but oval and this can be achieved by either bevelling down the existing horn, if sufficiently bulky, or by the use of some clamps or the dolly (*see* Chapter 10).

Ensure that the eyes are level before drilling. The fish eyes always seem rather large and bulbous and the best ones I have seen were made by filling the socket with glue then positioning an iris made of black buffalo in the middle, lightly pushing it in so that it is only just proud. This is smoothed down after the glue has set. Gills and fins are cut using either fine gouges, or an electric soldering iron or pyrography tool with a fine bit. The scales can be done with the same equipment but, if they are burnt in, the horn may melt slightly, resulting in a rather soft outline to the scales after sanding down. The best results are probably achieved with the gouge, used at approximately a 45-degree angle, lifting the horn slightly.

Colour wash before sanding down – felt pens are as good as anything – as this results in the scale outline being thrown into relief as the colour lodges in the gouge marks. If you prefer to have the mouth open slightly, cut carefully with a coping saw; alternatively, just define the line of the mouth with a fine gouge.

The traditional leaping trout handle is usually depicted with the tail in line with the body, adhering to the 'nose in line with neck' dictum. However, if realism is required, a far better version is achieved by having the tail twisted as it would be naturally when the fish is leaping. To do this, heat the tail and merely twist to the desired angle by hand, holding a cloth over it, if it is too hot, or gripping between two pieces of thin flat wood. Setting can be hastened by plunging in cold water. This is one subject where the best results are definitely obtained by having an actual fish as a model; it is difficult to do justice to trout simply from illustrations.

HALF-HEAD HANDLES

The half-head is a very popular stick in the North. It is a handle with only one bend – the heel – and consists simply of a neck and crown. The crown is carved in the shape of a bird or animal head: fox, badger, otter, dog, pheasant, partridge, grouse, duck, etc. It is very comfortable indeed, comes nicely to hand, and although fancy is not too elaborate to be carried as an everyday stick. It has the added advantages of not requiring a full-size horn to make the handle and being easier to make than the crook shape as it requires only one bend. Depending on

the bulk of the horn, it is often preferable to make this type 'back to front', the handle being shanked from the tip rather than the base of the horn. A good head will require no more than 8–10in (20–25cm) of horn. If there is a hollow portion, some squeezing up might be required.

Fox

A favourite subject, but not usually done well. The head will often look like that of an Alsatian dog or sometimes a Corgi, the colour anything from vermilion to pillar-box red – and these are show sticks! Unless one is an accomplished carver *and* familiar with the subject, a fox can be quite a difficult animal to which to do justice. The ears are not flush with the sides of the head but project marginally

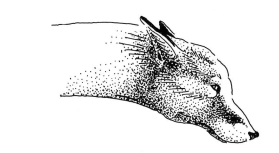

Good subjects for half-head handles: a fox and a horse.

69

Good subjects for half-head handles: a hound and a mallard.

beyond, neither do they face exactly forward but very slightly outwards. The forehead appears quite broad in contrast to the muzzle which is very narrow, tapering sharply from the neighbourhood of the eyes. The pupil in the eye is vertical. Before starting, it is better to study as many illustrations of the animal as possible, preferably from different angles. If you can study an actual fox mask, that would be better still.

Before committing oneself to the carving, it is sensible to mock up a scale model in plasticine. Once you are happy with it, you can start. It is much easier to omit the ears when carving as these are quite prominent and a good bulky horn would be required to carve out of the solid. Construct the ears from glue, thickened out with horn dust or fine shavings. Stick blobs of the mix in the area of the ears, leave until it begins to set (about two minutes) then roughly shape them using a small, flat screwdriver blade, a knife tip or

a wooden or plastic spatula. If there is not sufficient bulk of the mix to shape a full ear, it is an easy matter to add more. For strength, it may be advisable to fix in place three panel pins of suitable length, with the longest in the centre and the shorter ones on either side, slightly forward. This simplifies the ear building. The shape is finalized once the glue mixture is set. The fur can be textured using a sharpened electric soldering iron bit or equivalent pyrography tool. This melts the horn slightly and if rough can be lightly sanded down afterwards.

Badger

This is an easier subject than the fox. An older animal has a broad skull and a wedge-shaped head, with a shallow brow-line, and a rather blunt snout. The jaws and snout of a younger animal are not so pronounced. When painting, remember that the black and white facial pattern is not sharply defined but merged with grey shading. The ears are set fairly close to the skull and can be built up with the glue mix, as with the fox, if carving from the horn is impracticable. Similarly, texturing of the fur improves the carving considerably. This is a good subject in black buffalo horn as only the white and grey features require painting.

Duck

The mallard is probably the most common duck subject for a stick handle, but I have also seen wigeon, teal, pochard, and tufted duck (the latter is ideal for black buffalo horn). Again, study illustrations before starting and pay particular attention to the frontal view. All ducks have a narrow crown to the head with the cheek portion much broader. The eyes are set into a groove which is crescent shaped and roughly two-thirds of the length of the head. The beak of the mallard is approximately as long as the head, so the base ends roughly half-way between the tip of the beak and the back of the head. Other species have bills that are rather smaller in comparison. The graceful curves and proportions of ducks' heads lend themselves admirably to stick handles and the broad beaks are strong which is a necessity if the stick is to be used regularly. Feathering can be done with either a small gouge or a suitably shaped bit on a pyrography tool.

As a variation to duck handles, try a *swan* instead; the graceful lines make a very pleasing handle, and it is so much easier to paint.

Pheasant

This is probably the most commonly seen half-head in either wood or horn. The cock bird varies tremendously in colour and there is a fairly common melanistic strain which has the most beautiful, very dark head with striking feathering shot with purple. The wattles (or 'chollers' in the North) around the eye are larger, the older the bird. Probably the best size for this style is life-size so it is handy if you can obtain a good head to be kept in the freezer until needed. An older bird makes a better subject than a youngster, and I do not ever recall seeing a hen pheasant on a handle. If you are unable to obtain a good head, try to get a to-scale drawing which can be used as a template.

After heating, squeeze up the base of the horn either between two steel plates or the vice jaws, to a thickness of about 1¼in (3.2cm). This is the width of a normal

head so ensure that any rough spots, etc. on the sides of the horn have been removed beforehand as you will be needing clean horn to work with. Now mark out the head using the template or copying from an actual head. File or cut out the shape in profile, allowing a little extra fullness to the back of the head. Then file down the centre of the back of the head lengthways and undercut to shape the ears. If the beak area has a hollow over it, the surrounding area will need to be heated and squeezed up lightly. If this does not remove the hollow portion, a suitable piece of horn should be glued in place.

The head and neck can now be rounded off and smoothed down, then the 'chol-

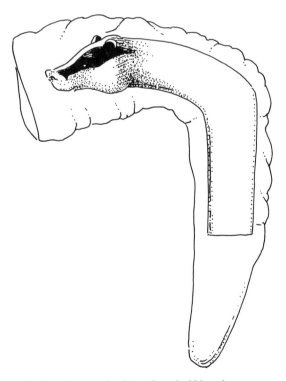

A badger is a good subject for a half-head handle. This one is to be shanked from the tip.

71

lers' should be marked in, using a template to ensure that both sides are similar. Drill holes for the eyes after pencilling in the position and levelling up as necessary. Glue in the eyes, cut from black buffalo horn. Mark the beak area, using either a soldering iron with a suitable bit or a fine gouge or 'V' parting tool. Smooth down again then feather the head and neck; a suitable gouge is best for this but feathering can be burned in with a shaped bit in a soldering iron or pyrography tool. It will be necessary to smooth down again before painting. One tip when painting: try not to make an even 'dog collar' around the neck (this also applies to the mallard drake) – aim instead for a rather uneven white line delineated by the feathering.

12 Horn Disc Sticks

A popular stick in Victorian times was made without any wood in its construction. This was the 'washer' or disc stick, constructed from a length of iron rod acting as a core upon which horn pieces were slotted; these numbered several hundred in some instances. You needed muscles to carry one of these sticks as even a short 3ft (1m) one could be upwards of 5lb (2kg) in weight. However, if you use a light alloy rod core and slot horn discs on to the handle, having only an ordinary shank, you can produce quite a pleasing and unusual stick.

You will need alloy rod, ⅜in (1cm) diameter; this is normally available in metre lengths. Allow 16–18in (40–45cm) for a crook handle, which includes 2in to be jointed into the shank. Allowing for these 2in (5cm), decide on a neck length (4–5in (10–12.5cm) is adequate) and mark it off. Smear soft soap around the area of the mark and heat with a blow lamp or hot-air gun. When the soap burns off, after two or three minutes, you should find that you can place the rod in a vice and bend the heated portion to the required shape for the heel. A fine spray of cold water will set this into position quickly. Repeat this process along the crown and with the nose, keeping in mind the eventual overall diameter of the handle when the discs are added.

The horn discs need to be slightly in excess of 1in (2.5cm) in diameter, although marginally smaller ones may be used towards the nose. It is not necessary to have them all similar in size as the final sanding down will make good any differences. Solid pieces can be drilled out through the centre. If using cow horn you will often find that this is hollow but with the hole suffering from 'converging verticals'. This does not matter too much as long as the hole is not too large or off-centre. I think that a dry run can be useful at this stage, mainly to obviate the possibility of a zebra effect where light- and dark-coloured horn discs alternate regularly. Also it is advisable to use discs of different thicknesses (though I never use any that are more than ½in (1.3cm) deep), to create a less formal effect, and a fair proportion of them will need to be cut wedge shaped to get around the curves of the heel and the nose.

When you are satisfied with the fit and colour range and the overall shape (the rod may need a little more work on it) slide all the discs off and put them in order on a length of dowel. Score the rod lightly along its length with a file to give a good

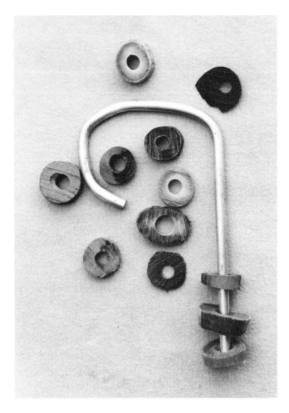

An alloy rod shaped to the market stick style, with horn discs.

proved by being one piece of horn – try to make this a good contrast. You will find that a nice tip of reddish cow horn or honey-coloured ram's horn looks particularly good. Try to keep the same diameter throughout the length of the handle with only a slight taper towards the tip. The 2in (5cm) protruding rod on the end can now be inserted into the shank but, as a safety measure and also to finish off nicely, place a horn collar around the joint. This should not be the same shade as the adjoining disc. Finally, sand down and finish in the normal way.

I have utilized the following horn in making these sticks and you will find that they give a good colour range: ram's horn, Highland cow, billy-goat, black buffalo, coloured buffalo, oxhorn and Nubian Ibex. You would be very fortunate if you obtained any Nubian Ibex. I found mine in a junk shop, mounted on a shield, with a date showing that it had been obtained ninety years ago. It had the most beautiful tortoiseshell-type horn when cut and polished after removing layers of old varnish.

key for the glue. Then slip on the discs sequentially, ensuring that both the rod and the flats of the discs are glued and pressed firmly together as they fall into position. Twist fit if necessary to get a better seat. With cow horn, you will find that the hole is rarely a good fit; have a glue and horn dust mixture ready to fill any such gaps but do not use this to joint the discs. The nose of the stick is im-

It might be thought that this type of horn disc handle will be rather heavy but actually this is not the case. The crook handle weighed 7oz (118g) and the market stick 4oz (140g) and these are near enough similar to traditional horn handles of comparative shape and size.

One final word of warning: if you want to make one of these sticks you are going to need an awful lot of glue.

13 Assembling the Stick

FITTING HANDLE TO SHANK

It goes without saying that the handle should be of the same dimensions as the shank, wherever feasible. Certainly this applies to wood or horn handles which can be shaped to size but with antler this is often not possible. Never have a handle that is too small in girth for the shank – it will never look right. On the other hand, one that is marginally larger can usually be made to look acceptable if bevelled off smoothly down to the joint. A collar will also usually help to camouflage any discrepancy.

There are various methods of jointing the handle to the shank and, if the stick is meant for shows, any of them will suffice. But if the stick is to have any practical use, it is necessary to have as strong a joint as possible. The poorest method that I have seen which dates from Victorian times is by Dover screw. This is simply a double-ended screw (no head), about 2in (5cm) long which is screwed into the handle and then the shank. This joint has no strength even though it is glued. Another type uses a 4, 5 or 6in (10, 12·5 or 15cm) nail with the head cut off. The nail is simply fitted into holes drilled in both handle and

shank and glued. Again, this has very little strength: it is possible to bend the mild steel of these nails between the fingers easily, which does not augur well for the stick if used regularly. One favoured method is to use a length of studding, which is mild-steel-threaded rod, ¼–⅜in (0·6–1cm) in diameter. Suitable holes are bored in both handle and shank and the rod inserted after being glued.

I do not like to introduce metal into horn, antler or wood as the marriage will not be as permanent as a wood dowel joint. Rather than use commercial dowels simply shape a dowel on the top of the shank. First, drill a hole in the handle of a depth of no more than 1in (2·5cm), using a spade or a flat bit in a power tool. I have a selection of these from ½in (1·3cm) up to ⅞in (2·2cm) and these cover all eventualities. The sharp point on this drill is a good lead-in when commencing drilling and prevents the drill from wandering, also it is easy to find the centre point. It is a popular misconception that a long dowel is essential for strength but in fact 1in is ample. Leave a rim around the drilled hole of about ⅛in if it is horn or antler but rather more if a wood handle is used. Measure the depth of the hole; a nail is ideal for this. Holding your thumb on the nail as a guide to the hole depth, put it against the top of the stick and make a scratch mark on the bark at the required distance. If the shank is holly or blackthorn, try to avoid a length that contains knots as they will make the dowelling difficult.

Lay the stick loosely along the top of the vice with the jaws open only about ½in (1·3cm), which is sufficient to hold the stick slightly and, using a coping saw, start at the scratch mark and circle the stick sawing through the bark just enough to lightly score the wood. Hold the stick under one arm and, using a sharp knife, bring the blade back into the saw cut and lightly skin off the bark towards the end of the stick. Continue all round the stick. Look at the stick from the trimmed end

The four stages in dowelling: (left to right) mark length with a saw cut; trim away from the saw cut; trim back to the saw cut to remove cone shape; trim to fit.

and you will see if it is round in section, allowing for the knife cuts. Remove any oval shape or prominent flats using the knife, cutting towards oneself and aiming for as near a round trimmed section as possible. Hold up the stick at eye level and you will see that the dowel shape does not have parallel sides as it should, but is slightly cone shaped, caused by the knife blade cutting into the bark at a slight angle from the saw cut. Level off the sides of the dowel now by bringing the knife blade down gently from about half-way down the dowel towards the rim of the saw cut. After this stage, the dowel should be reasonably shaped. Now try it for size in the handle and repeat the foregoing stages until a twist fit (not a push fit) is achieved.

When you are satisfied that the dowel is a reasonably tight fit (do not try to force it into a wood handle as the dowel will act like a wedge and break the sides of the drilled handle), ensure that it is sitting properly on the shank. Occasionally the dowel will be slightly too long for the depth of the hole drilled but it is a simple matter to shorten to the correct length. Twist the handle round the shank until the best seat is found – there is always one place where the handle sits well – and run a pencil or ball-pen mark down from the handle on to the shank to mark the spot. Before glueing, score the dowel lengthways a few times with the knife point which allows surplus glue to escape down to the joint, otherwise there would be a small cushion of glue at the head of the dowel and the handle would not sit firmly at the joint. Any dowel which is not a good firm twist fit can have a small wedge part inserted in the end which will be driven home to expand the dowel slightly when the handle is fitted.

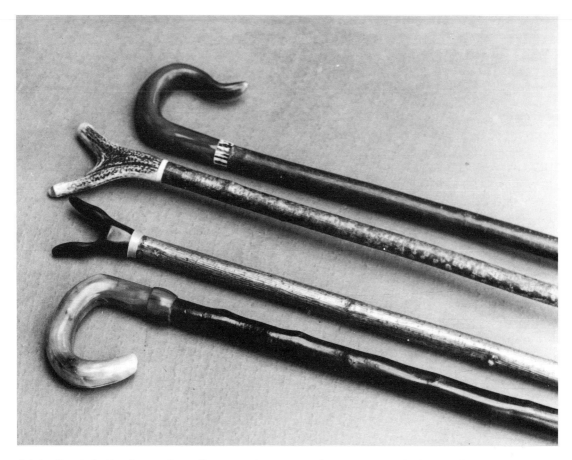

Joints: (top to bottom) an antler collar; an antler spacer; a horn spacer and a horn collar.

Finally, smear glue around the sides and the end of the dowel and fix the handle in position by twisting until the pen/pencil marks are lined up. Wipe off the surplus glue from the joint. A good tight fit is assured if a length of ladies' nylon stocking or tights is slipped over the handle after glueing, pulled down tightly to hold in position, and tied down until set. Care must be taken not to pull the handle down at an angle but this can be noticed through the nylon and tension adjusted accordingly. Epoxy glues are the most effective for fixing handles to shanks.

Any stick that is to be used regularly, particularly in rough or hill country where one's weight will bear down on it frequently, should have a collar around the joint to add to the strength. That apart, they can be decorative, although that description does not apply to the metal collars which can occasionally be seen. Collars can be either antler or horn and are most effective when standing proud of the handle and shank. Simply obtain a 1in (2·5cm) length of antler or horn (cow horn is particularly nice if you have it), with a diameter slightly bigger than that of the joint. Drill out the collar and open up to the necessary width with a round rasp. I find a piece of coarse emery wrapped around a ½in (1·3cm) dowel to be useful here. When a twist fit is achieved, slide the collar 1in (2·5cm) up the handle (*not* the shank as it may slide down due to the taper) then glue up the dowel in the normal way and joint shank and handle. Smear glue around the joint, roughly ½in (1·3cm) on either side, and slide the collar down into position. Remove any surplus glue. When set, bevel down the top and bottom of the collar to give a barrel shape but before doing this it is as well to bind insulating tape or Sellotape around both shank and handle adjacent to the collar to prevent marking. Do not have a collar standing too proud, ⅛in (0·3cm) is all that is required.

If you do not intend to use a stick regularly, a purely decorative spacer or disc of horn or antler can be inserted between the handle and the shank. Cut out a suitable piece and drill out using the same size drill as the dowel. When measuring the depth of the drilled hole in the handle, an addition must be made for the thickness of the spacer prior to measuring out the dowel length. Simply rest the collar on the drilled out handle and measure the overall depth. If you would like a more decorative spacer try a tricolour. Use a dark horn (buffalo), followed by a light horn (ram's horn), followed by a dark horn again, or alternatively place a piece of dark horn between two pieces of light horn. All three need to be glued together of course.

There is a fashion amongst some stickmakers for making a slanting joint but I do not see an awful lot of point to them. They are certainly not an improvement on the traditional horizontal joint and do not really justify the extra effort expended in shaping them. I have also seen a zigzag joint but this was some flight of fancy of the maker and did nothing to improve the look of the stick. Such a joint would in fact detract from a good horn head. Leonard Parkin once showed me a dovetail jointed stick and this was only done as a challenge to the maker's skill and ingenuity. It would be impossible to do this with any other kind of handle but horn and was achieved by carefully measuring and cutting out the dovetails in both shank and handle. Then the dovetails on the handle were heated and bent out at an angle, the handle and shank glued and brought together and the horn dovetails glued and brought back into line to marry with those on the shank. Finally, to hold in position until set, a jubilee clip was tightened around the joint. Quite a challenge!

FITTING FERRULE TO SHANK

The ferrule is fitted to the tip of the shank to prevent undue wear and tear. It can also be fitted to a show stick, which will never be used, but I feel that in these circumstances it is superfluous. The most practical kind for the type of stick that will be in everyday use is a length of brass or copper pipe. I prefer a 2in (5cm) ferrule, as a short one results in the bark immediately above it becoming badly worn and frayed with use. It is not essential to be flush with the shank, ie. the same diameter, and it is quite acceptable for it to stand proud. Fixing is not difficult – simply trim the tip of the shank to the required length for the piece of pipe to be tapped into position, after the trimmed portion has been glued. Remember that glue has a slightly lubricating effect so a tight fit is required initially. When fitted, I hammer a dome-headed nail, trimmed to a length of 1in (2·5cm) into the end of the shank until just the head is showing. This prevents the metal ferrule wearing at an angle.

Purely decorative ferrules can be made from horn or antler but although it may be thought that, as these make excellent hard-wearing handles, they should also make good ferrules, this is not the case. Horn will wear out surprisingly quickly if in regular contact with the ground, particularly if stony, and antler will almost certainly shatter if bumped against stones frequently. Fit these type of ferrules to show sticks by all means but do not be tempted to use them on an ordinary working stick. Always glue a ferrule into position as wood expands and contracts depending on its moisture content and many a ferrule has been lost after a long spell of hot dry weather. Rubber ferrules are available commercially but these are not very hard-wearing and are a positive menace on wet rock. However, if you wish to do bird or animal watching, and

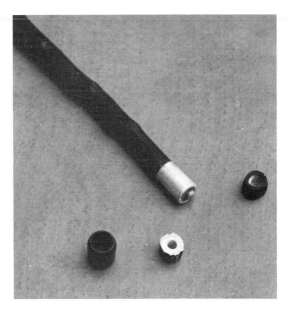

Ferrules: (left to right) rubber; antler; copper pipe; horn.

so need to go quietly, then this is the best type to use. As they tend to flex considerably in use and become loose, tap a ½in (1·3cm) carpet tack through the side wall of the rubber into the stick to prevent loss.

14 Finishing

The finish of a stick is all-important and one that is poorly finished is a reproach to its owner. Before the polishing stage is reached, a few simple steps can be undertaken to improve the final result. The bark on a hazel is often flaky on the surface but a light rub-down with steel wool will reveal the true colour underneath. Ash is invariably coarse to the touch and needs similar treatment. Blackthorn, hawthorn and holly should have the knots standing proud, not dressed down flush with the shank, and these should be sanded smooth without scratch marks. Any checks in the knobs look better filled, which will also serve to strengthen the shank as they may run deeply; use glue then sprinkle with the appropriate wood dust. A careful smoothing down of the debarked shank is essential for holly as otherwise every scratch will be prominent once the white wood is stained. However, do not smooth down the bare wood with steel wool, nor the head of a block stick or any plain wood head, as specks of the wool will lodge in the wood to rust later and 'run a stain'.

I never use sandpaper, which is too expensive and also brittle, making it shred quickly. Use emery cloth wrapped around a cork or rubber block for sanding or make up several blocks in the following way: sandwich pieces of wood, measuring 4in (10cm) by 1½in (3.8cm) by ½in–¾in (1.3–1.9cm), between firm foam rubber, stretch emery around it, and tack it down. Start with a 40-grit (coarse), then 80-grit (medium), finishing with 120-grit (fine). Lengths of dowel, made up in similar fashion, ¾in (1.9cm) thick, are ideal for the difficult inside curves on handles. Emery cloth is also employed to make strapping which is simply a 1in (2.5cm) strip pulled from a sheet of the abrasive, used two-handed for strapping purposes. If there are marks in the wood which are rather stubborn, I find that using the strapping one-handed with a thumb pressed down on it over the part to be smoothed works very quickly. Strapping is perfect for keeping all the contours rounded. It must not just be pulled to and fro, but also slightly sideways, otherwise grooving will occur. A light tap on the work-bench will clear the abrasive when it clogs up with dust. Although 120-grit will ostensibly remove most scratches, you will find that, with horn in particular, it will in fact leave a network of fine hair-line marks. To remove these use finer grade, up to 600-grit, known also as 'flour paper'. This is normally 'wet and dry' and paper backed and does not clog too easily if used wet. The sludge it creates looks messy but wipes off readily.

Antler, although heavily grooved as a rule, benefits from a light sanding down – this will also bring out a nice mottle on a dark piece – followed by polishing with either car-rubbing paste or a liquid metal cleaner. There is nothing to choose between them as they both contain a very fine abrasive powder, suspended in paste in one and in liquid in the other. Rub in vigorously with a cloth in each case followed, after a brief interval, by a polish with another cloth. You will often find a powdery deposit in the antler grooves afterwards but this can easily be removed with an old tooth brush. Horn will benefit from more than one application of the polish to bring out the lustrous sheen that is its hallmark, and any fine scratches can easily be seen as the powder lodges in them. Remove them using wet and dry before repolishing.

Varnish will give a superficially attractive finish to a stick (although it looks superfluous on ash with its rather homely grey-green bark) but the stick you see resplendent in its single coat of polyurethane hard-glaze finish will not look so pristine in a year if used regularly. The gloss finish will be marked with chips, scratches and cracks, where the stick has flexed in use, and dirt will have entered these and left unsightly marks. If the stick has been well used in bramble, bracken or other rough areas, the bottom 3–4in (7.5–10cm) will probably be devoid of varnish and the bark beginning to wear off. The handle too will have lost its gloss, owing to the abrasive action of your palm.

The best finish is undoubtedly obtained from the regular use of linseed oil. Nothing can match the burnished glow on a

Rubber-cushioned emery-covered dowels. Dog chews wrapped around with emery are also useful.

wood handle or the beauty of the bark on a shank, brought out by repeated applications of linseed oil and regular use of this prolongs the natural resilience of the wood to a far greater extent than varnish can. Polish with a soft rag, rubbing in vigorously. Oiled regularly, your stick will visibly improve with age, and the palm of your hand will polish the handle. Linseed oil can also be used on both horn and antler. I find no difference between raw linseed and boiled. The raw kind is supposed to contain impurities which prevent it from setting hard but in practice I have found that this is fallacious. Any tackiness will always disappear after brisk rubbing with a dry cloth. How often should you use linseed? Follow the advice of the old North Country saying and you will not go far wrong:

> Once a day for a week,
> Once a week for a month,
> Once a month for a year,
> And once a year for life.

15 Miniature Sticks

In 1989, following a proposal I had made earlier, the British Stickmakers' Guild introduced a class for miniature sticks at their stick shows. These have proved very popular both with stickmakers and the public in general. The class is for a set of five sticks, either plain or fancy, in any material, and in any style, mounted on a base of the maker's choice. The maximum length is 9in (23cm) including the handle and they should, of course, be in the correct proportions. The scope for making these miniatures is limitless bearing in mind the specification, but although in

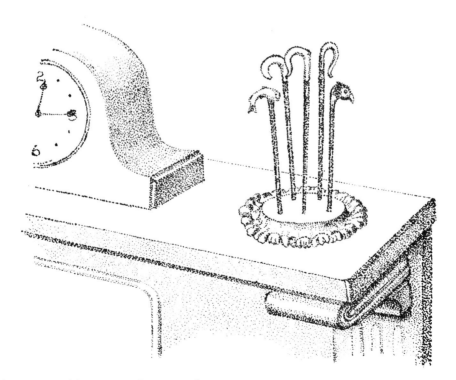

A set of miniature sticks on an antler coronet base.

theory they could be made from man-made material such as Tufnol or cast resin, stickmakers have remained faithful to the materials they habitually use: wood, horn and antler.

By far the nicest sets that I have seen have been true, scaled-down versions of the full-sized article with horn heads. A typical set would comprise a thumb stick, a walking or market stick, a crook, a leg crook, and a ram's curl. I feel that they look best when the handles are all of the same kind of horn as mixing different types produces rather a jumbled effect. The shanks have been rather a mixed bunch of dowels, turned hardwood, trim-med down hazel, holly, ash or blackthorn stick pieces, and even twigs complete with bark. Some have been plain and others stained. Handles have usually been pinned (a 1in (2·5cm) nail minus the head being the most popular) or dowel-led, that is with the end of the shank being fashioned into a dowel which is fitted into the handle.

A common base has been a piece of horn or an antler coronet, but I have seen a polished hardwood block, a chunk of elm burr, a mounted wood crook handle with holes around the crown to hold the sticks, and a small ram's horn lying on its side with the sticks mounted on the curled portion. I have a set mounted on a curved base of polished horn set into a cedar wood cigar box standing on end, and am toying with the idea of fitting a piece of mirror glass behind the sticks with a view to possibly enhancing their appeal. A set makes an unusual table ornament or fits nicely on a cabinet, book shelf or mantelpiece. They are an ideal present for any country lover, and can be parcelled up and sent through the post easily. They do not pose any great difficul-ties in construction require no elaborate workshop set-up and are a worthwhile project for any enthusiastic stickmaker.

THE SHANK

The easiest way to make the shank is by using commercially made dowels, usually beech or ramin. Both are straight grained and fairly uninteresting. If you own a miniature lathe, virtually any type of hardish wood can be used but, by choice, I would use yew, juniper or blackthorn, the first two for their rich colouring, and the latter because the spines run right into the wood to the centre and can leave an interesting burr when smoothed down. I dislike twigs as shanks as they are rarely straight and, possibly because of the sap content, the bark wrinkles easily. They also have a considerable pith which makes them rather brittle when seasoned. I have found that a suitable shank can be made fairly easily by selecting a seasoned length of holly or blackthorn for prefer-ence. Split with a sharp knife lengthways down the middle, then split each half again giving you four quarter round lengths. If the grain is twisted longitudi-nally in the wood you will almost certainly have a distortion as you cut and I would discard these lengths as being too much trouble to work. Again with your knife, whittle away carefully at each length trying initially to round off the cut faces and next to remove the bark. Finally, buff each shank with emery cloth and fine down to the necessary diameter, bearing in mind that a slight taper along the length is to be aimed for. If any are bent slightly, straighten in your fingers. Once straightened, they should remain that way. A coffee stain can be added as

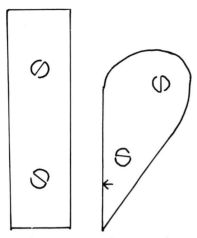

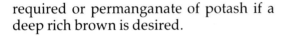

A template for a nose-in style mini stick.

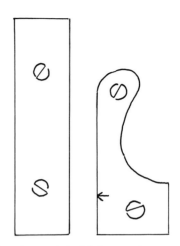

A template for a mini stick leg crook.

required or permanganate of potash if a deep rich brown is desired.

THE HANDLE

I have made a thumb stick piece from the end two tines of a yearling roe-buck antler and experimented with odd wood crooks and a variety of handle styles but most exponents of the craft would agree that by far the best miniature sticks have horn handles. There are two methods of making these. The easiest is by drawing the handle shape on a flat sheet of horn approximately ¼in (0·6cm) thick. This can be a slice of ram's horn or buffalo horn, sawn lengthways, or a length of hollow cow horn, cut down the middle, heated for a minute with a hot-air gun or hair-dryer, flattened in the vice jaws and allowed to set for five minutes. Cut out the shape using a fine-bladed coping saw, trying for a handle size marginally larger than drawn and being particularly careful to avoid overcutting where the inside of the crown meets the neck as the saw changes direction. A thumb piece need

only be cut out as a crude triangle as the neck and the opening for the thumb is easily shaped using needle files. You will now have square-edged handle shapes, which require rounding.

The outer edges can be shaped with emery wrapped around a cork, or rubber block for preference and worked with the grain as far as possible. The inside curves particularly are rather more difficult and I have found the easiest way of tackling these is by using a ¼in (0·6cm) diameter length of dowel wrapped in emery. Re-place this dowel with a smaller one or a nail when shaping the leg crook inside curves which are much narrower than the crook shape. If you are making a ram's curl handle, cut out as for a market stick with nose in. The neck and crown are identical to the market stick but the length of the nose is twisted backwards and outwards into a curl. The nose should be heated and carefully curled around a piece of suitable dowel or a pencil and held in place with a pair of tweezers if too hot to hold. A squirt of cold water will speed up the setting time.

The second method of making horn

handles is virtually identical to that used in making standard size sticks in so far as it consists of utilizing lengths of horn which are heated and then formed around templates. You will require lengths of horn (running with the grain) from 3–4in (7·5–10cm) long and approximately ¼in sq (0·6cm sq) for each handle shape except the thumb piece, which can be cut out of a piece of horn as described in the first method. Three templates are required for the other four handle shapes: a market stick with nose in, which doubles for making the ram's curl style; a narrow leg crook; and a standard crook. Cut these out of ½in (1·3cm) thick hardwood and then fix by glueing and/or nailing to a baseboard, placing them at least 2in (5cm) apart. Parallel to the neck of each template, affix a further oblong piece of ½in (1·3cm) thick hardwood, approximately ¼in

(0·6cm) away, to form a channel in which one end of the heated horn is placed with the remainder bent into shape around the template and held in position with a few ½ or ¾in (1·3 or 2cm) panel pins tapped into the baseboard. Leave until set then round off as before, with the ram's curl style being shaped as previously.

JOINTING

You should now have shanks and handles of approximately 3/16in (0·5cm) in diameter and jointing such small items needs

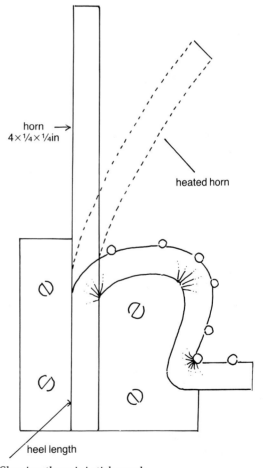

A template for a mini stick crook.

Shaping the mini stick crook.

care. If the dowel method is used, drill a suitable hole in the handle using a hand drill but ensure that such a small drill bit is held firmly in the chuck. If it does not seem to be gripped fast, insert the drill bit in a fibre rawlplug which should make it fit the drill chuck tightly enough. Make a drill stop ½in (1·3cm) from the tip of the drill by wrapping a length of Sellotape or insulating tape around the drill. This ensures that you do not drill too deeply into the neck of the handle. Hold the handle in a small vice, preferably with wood or fibre jaw inserts to prevent marking the horn, and try to ensure that the drill is held as vertical as possible. Mark off the shank ½in (1·3cm) from the end and try to avoid any knots in the wood if using holly or blackthorn as they are extremely hard and even the sharpest blade is liable to snag on them when making the dowel. Once the shank is dowelled, twist fit the handle into position ensuring that it sits properly. Mark this position with a pencil-line near the joint down from the horn on to the shank and line up the two marks when glueing up. Use epoxy glue smeared on the dowel and wipe away surplus glue around the joint then prop up the completed stick to dry. You may find a razor blade more suitable than a knife for dowelling.

If you prefer to pin the handle to the shank, you will need to drill both. The major point in favour of this method is that if either (or both) holes have not been drilled truly vertical, the head will not sit right but the pin can easily be bent slightly to ensure a better fit. This would not be possible if the dowel method was used. Glue up each half of the pin before insertion into the handle and the shank

and again clear surplus glue away before it sets.

THE BASE

A reasonably sized antler coronet makes a good setting for miniature sticks. Smooth down the rough crown of the coronet then mark, with pencil, five holes – I prefer a loose W-shaped formation, which I feel sets off the sticks better than a plain fan shape with the five all in line. Hold each stick in turn on to the pencil mark appropriate to it then drill a hole approximately ½in (1·3cm) deep and at the appropriate angle. If the angle turns out to be slightly wrong – and this is often the case – open up the drilled hole slightly to correct the imbalance, using either the drill pulled slightly sideways or a round or half-round needle file. This will probably result in a loose fit for the stick so push a small piece of putty into the hole and set the stick at the right angle then withdraw and allow the putty to harden. When the sticks have been mounted to your satisfaction, the whole setting can be finished using a fine paintbrush and clear varnish or lacquer, with care taken to ensure that there are no drips or runs. A felt base can be affixed if required.

The scope for imagination in deciding the base style is unlimited and this also applies to the handle style but here the constraints of working in miniature dictate the choice. Although it is possible to carve and paint a pheasant head or trout, for instance, the final results, with the inevitable loss of detail and the sheer lack of impact in the miniature format, do not really justify the effort.

16 Shows and Judging

The judge, who fancied himself as a bit of a character, stood at the far side of the stick rack facing the rapt audience. He looked across the massed display of sticks and, catching someone's eye, said 'Hey, Jonty, didn't see ye there. Happen ye'll have some in today?'

'Aye', came the reply, as he pointed, 'That one next ye, and them'ns there.' Needless to say, Jonty was amongst the tickets that day. This might appear a blatant example of favouritism or even downright dishonesty as the sticks are identified by numbers only and judges are, in theory at least, not supposed to know the makers. But I have known a judge travel to a show with one of the competitors and I do not suppose for one moment that they spent the journey discussing the scenery. If experienced, most judges will have seen a fair number of the sticks previously at other shows and, that apart, can recognize certain individual styles in any case. And do not imagine that all judges are selected for their knowledge of sticks; they may be friends or relations of a show committee member who have been roped in to help, or the proprietor of a trade stand who may sell sticks and who has been asked for no other reason than that he is already at the show and so no travelling expenses need be paid. I have also seen a local MP officiating at one show and a locally born radio/TV personality judging at another. Both looked as if they had never handled a stick in their lives but at least, for once, both were virtually bereft of speech.

However, the dedicated stickmaker who enters his sticks in shows regularly must look upon such events with equanimity as part and parcel of competing. Even the best stickmaker in the country would never win more than half of the shows he entered, owing to the fallibility and quite often even the ignorance of the judges and their own particular preferences and dislikes. The canny stickmaker's creed should always be 'horses for courses' – when choosing which sticks to enter, bear in mind local preferences and any of those of the judges that are known. In the Lake District, for instance, where there are six packs of foxhounds and thousands of sheep, sticks depicting a fox, hound or terrier, and a lamb, ewe, ram or collie dog, either individually or in various permutations, always do well. Northumberland and Durham have a long tradition of fancy dressed sticks and trout, pheasant and adder are amongst local favourites. The round heel on a crook predominates in Northumberland whereas the square heel is always used in the Border areas, and either style is acceptable in the Lake District.

If the judge is a fisherman, a salmon or trout-headed stick should impress and if he is a shooting man, offer up a pheasant or grouse. Even then you will still have to face personal idiosyncrasies – some judges hate snakes, others dislike oval shanks. I know of one who cannot abide the black streaks which are common in some ram's horn and one who dislikes blackthorn shanks, however attractive, because he considers them to be 'too heavy'. Another thinks that a ram's horn showing the pinkish tinge in parts, caused by blood diffusion, is a poor horn and marks down accordingly. This is nonsense, of course, but unfortunately it is he who is the judge. One will not even consider black buffalo horn – 'this new-fangled stuff' – disregarding the fact that ram's horn is now so difficult to obtain that buffalo is the only reasonable alternative.

The judge at one Lake District show, a local hill shepherd who liked a good firm stick, caused consternation amongst some of the competitors when he held each stick by the handle with the point on the ground and pressed down very hard in the middle of the shank. If it gave by more than 1in (2·5cm) it was rejected. However, by far the worst kind of judge is, without a doubt, the one (and he is by no means rare) who does not handle the sticks, pausing at each class only for such time as it takes him to indicate his choice to the steward. Every stick should be handled, irrespective of merit. How else can one see the shank? Aprt from it being a fallacy that a stick can be judged solely by looking at it, the owner has expended

care, skill and time on it and the judge should respect that.

Of course, in every class there are sticks where the maker is obviously a firm believer in the dictum that it is better to travel hopefully than to arrive, so poor is their quality. None the less, their work may happen to be in a class where the standard is low and theirs could just have that extra edge. This happens regularly at the smaller shows, particularly if the date of the show clashes with a larger and more popular one that attracts all the best makers, although some of the more enthusiastic ones have been known to send half of their sticks to a minor show with a friend whilst competing elsewhere themselves. It is only by making an honest appraisal of one's own work in direct comparison with that of others that personal standards can be raised. It is not much good thinking – or saying – that you have better sticks at home, unless you are prepared to prove it by entering competitions. If you do take part, then remember the Olympic ideal of the honour lying in taking part rather than winning. However, it does give great pleasure to earn a rosette, so how does one set about making show sticks?

It goes without saying that a certain measure of skill is required in making fancy sticks to show, but skills can be acquired or improved upon and if you are not a carver you can still be good at copying. Quite a few of the pheasant head, trout and adder sticks that are seen at shows have been created from the original, which has been kept in a freezer until required. They are painstakingly reproduced in wood or horn with precise measurements by caliper and rule and each scale or feather accurately depicted and coloured. But often the results will

Show day.

still not be very lifelike, the pheasant looking rather rigid and the trout, stiff and unnatural. The trouble is that they have been copied from dead objects; the pheasant with that slight kink in the neck, or head marginally to one side, at just that instant of alertness when it had spotted the worm, or the trout with its tail flicked slightly sideways as it leaps to catch the fly, are both infinitely more life-like than the freezer model versions.

It hardly need be added that authenticity of detail should also be aimed for: a woodpecker, for instance, has two toes before and two behind yet I have often seen one on a fancy carved stick with three before and one behind as this is how birds' feet are more commonly formed. A nuthatch depicted running up a trunk always seems to be not quite right as this species is noted for its habit of running down. Foxes and collie dogs habitually carry their heads no higher than their shoulders but are often depicted with them higher. Sheep ears grow in the main at right angles to the head and are very prominent yet are not always shown to be so. I can even remember one fine horn crook with a beautifully detailed belligerent-looking ram with prominent horns but with the ears missing altogether. Some makers will go to extraordinary lengths, such as making the teeth on a snarling badger head from lengths of coping saw blade. I have also seen a pair of real legs from a dead specimen fixed to a carved blue tit but, unfortunately, the bird was not to scale.

Speaking as a judge, the finish of a good proportion of sticks leaves much to be desired. One often sees where varnish has run or a joint that is seemingly smooth being anything but when felt. I handled one stick which was still tacky from recently applied varnish and another where the shank had seen a lot of wear and was without bark for about 2in (5cm) up from the tip, which was without a ferrule (not that I feel that ferrules are essential to a show stick, which is not going to be used). It is a fact that many sticks which would win at a show if racked inside a marquee would most decidedly not if they were judged outside as happens at some shows. On a fine day, and particularly if the sun is at a diagonal angle, any faults in the finish, or dents and scratches, which would probably evade notice under canvas, are thrown into sharp relief.

Although there are no set rules for making sticks, there are some unwritten ones and these are often broken. The nose should not droop on a crook or market stick, nor even on a plain walking stick, neither should it be out of line with the shank when viewed from the front, nor should it be lower than the joint, although this seems to be permissible with a leg crook. A thistle on a crook should not lean in to the nose, nor lean out: it should be vertical. The crown of a stick should not be rat-tailed (i.e. taper drastically from the heel along towards the nose), but should be approximately the same diameter or marginally thicker along its length. Many sticks are perfectly good ones for everyday use but they are not up to show stick standard.

The final choice for a judge can be a difficult one, particularly in the plain-horn classes. One can be faced with upwards of a dozen sticks differing in finish, shank, and type of horn, but basically similar. Here the winner could well be the one made of horn that is not seen too often: Jacob's, for instance, or billy goat or Highland cow. With the fancy classes the choice, though it seems bewildering, can actually be much easier, as in the final analysis it is going to be one's own personal preference.

I like a touch of individuality as the vast majority of show sticks are too stereotyped. I would settle for the mouse with its tail curled around the crook nose, or the fox running up the nose with just the rear part of the rabbit disappearing down the hole at the front of the crown; they are the sort to command attention and win shows. The best sticks are detailed realistically but a broadly stylized one, which has a certain something about it, can be an eye-catcher too.

One could say, a trifle cynically, that the good judge is always the one who awards the rosettes to your sticks, whilst the bad one hardly gives them a look. If you think that all the agonizing and recriminations about results is confined to the men, just take a stroll around the show when the winners of the home-made jams and sponge cakes become known! If you are to show sticks regularly you will require, apart from a modicum of skill, patience, perseverance, a determination not to be upset by palpably unfair results and, above all, a sense of humour. You should be out to enjoy yourself, and you might have a long drive home afterwards which will seem twice as long if you are grieving over some injustice. It is nice to bask in the modest prestige of winning but it would be boring if it happened every time – or would it?

Appendix

TEN TIPS

1. However careful you are with your wood and horn handles (antler is not a problem in this respect), at some time or another they will suffer from dents. Two well tried remedies are using a hot iron and damp cloth or a warm to hot soldering iron and felt. Wood will need sanding down afterwards to remove any 'whiskers' whilst horn will require repolishing.

2. If you are using a horn capping on an antler handle, or simply adding a carved item to a fancy stick, the joint can be made more secure if a few fine holes are drilled beforehand, both in the cut edges of the handle and the piece to be added. The glue will fill these holes when jointed and form tiny pillars or pins of adhesive, thus adding extra strength to the joint.

3. Preventing the white from surfacing is a problem that faces every horn-head maker. It is compounded by the annoying tendency of the white to be neither in the middle of the horn, nor near to either the inner or outer curve of the handle, with any degree of regularity. However, if the horn is sufficiently smooth and dressed down with oil it is usually possible, when held up closely to a light, to see the white, which will show up darkly against the semi-translucent horn. Steps can then usually be taken to obviate the problem.

4. Six hours is an average time to spend on the feathering of a pheasant head or the scaling of a trout head handle. This time can be shortened considerably by making a semi-automatic tool especially for the task. Purchase a spring punch. Grind flat the point and shape a U or crescent using a round needle file. A larger U-shape or crescent can be had by grinding down further the tapered point. This point is retractable and tension can be varied with a simple turn of the knurled barrel and, if required, a stronger spring can easily be fitted.

5. It is very annoying to have a good ram's horn with a hole bored through. Usually this is towards the tip but often far enough from the end to make it impractical to trim the horn above it. However, I would suggest that, if the hole does not close up after heating and squeezing, a feature be made of it. Open up the hole a further inch (2·5cm)

lengthways. Then carve, insert and glue into place a horn fish, for example, within the limitations set by the size of the aperture. This results in rather an interesting handle.

6. The bark in holly shanks contains a rather pungent oil or sap. This is irresistible to field mice (or wood mice as they are now called) who have the sagacity to seek warmer quarters in winter-time and can often be found in greenhouses, sheds and outbuildings. If you have any holly sticks standing seasoning in these buildings you will often find that the bottom few inches have been bark stripped. This would not be so bad if it were only the bark, which you would be removing yourself when making up the shanks, but unfortunately there are quite often deep teeth marks in the wood. I have found that the only solution is to suspend the sticks by a thick cord

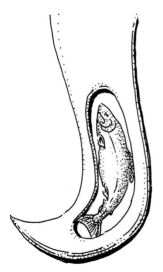

The existing hole in the nose of a horn has been enlarged and a miniature fish inserted making a feature of a fault.

from a cross-beam. Mice are extremely agile and would actually have no trouble in reaching these sticks but they appear to be unable to identify them overhead. They never bother nibbling any other kind of stick.

7. If you are short of antler for a spacer between handle and shank, use bone instead. Get some shin of beef from the butcher, remove all the marrow to prevent yellowing, scrape clean and then boil up with a biological washing powder (*not* bleach). When fitted, you will have an attractive white spacer. If you want a black spacer but have no buffalo horn, a perfect substitute, which is indistinguishable from horn when polished, is ebonite or vulcanite. This is made up from a compound of carbon and rubber, and can be obtained from most gunshops, particularly if they do repairs as it is used for capping gun butts. It is sold in blocks of various sizes around the 6in (15cm) length. Sand down as if it were horn and the end result is identical. It is perfect for topping cut edges on handles or for fish, bird and animal eyes. A further option is to make a spacer from leather. It works well, resists scratching, and improves with age, and can be black or shades of brown, or easily stained to any colour.

8. If you are faced with a dent, hole or crack in either wood or horn, which requires filling, instead of the usual mixture of glue and wood or horn dust, experiment instead with clear plastic casting resin. Clean out the base of the concavity first as this will be 'projected' to the surface by

the resin. It is sometimes advisable to build up a rampart of putty first to hold the liquid resin in position. A repair made in this way can be virtually impossible to detect.

9. The simplest way to unclog the dust from a sanding disc in a power tool (where there is still some abrasive left) is to run a brass bristle brush over it a few times. If the dust is obstinate, try 'sanding' a crunched-up polythene bag or the rough side of a piece of old boot leather. This will lift out the dust. If you use flap wheels in the power tool and these have become frayed and are losing their effectiveness, they can be given a new lease of life by running them a few times (in the drill) over a coarse rasp.

10. After spending a long time bending, shaping and carving a pheasant or mallard drake head it is often disappointing, when doing the final painting, not to be able to reproduce the brilliant sheen of the head feathers. This is impossible to depict accurately, whatever paint is used, but it is now possible to obtain iridescent powder, made from dyed bronze or

But why do sheep not shed their horns every year?

The stickmaker's dream.

aluminium, which gives near-perfect results. This is mixed with diluted clear glazing medium and applied in the same way as normal paint (it is best to have a trial run beforehand). Colours available are usually royal blue, violet, and emerald green and all should be stored in the dark to prevent fading. It is available from craft shops.

Index

Note: The page numbers of illustrations are indicated in *italic* type.

abrasives, 17, 20, 26, 34, 62, 78, 80, 93
Ash, 9, 12, 14, 23, 24, 31, 33, 34, 80–1, 83, 84

balance, 9, 10, 11, 21, 30, 32, 66
bending
   wood, 23–4
   antler, 36
   horn, 15, 51, 52, 53, 54, 56–63, 68, 69, 84, 85
billy-goat horn, 51–2, 63
blackthorn, 10, 11, 12, 13, 14, 21, 23, 24, 25, 27,
   28, 29, 30, 33, 76, 83, 86, 88
block sticks, 14, 23, 25–7, 29
blowlamp, 18, 25, 36, 56, 73
bone, 19, 36, 43, 92
buffalo horn
   black, 28, 52, 62, 63–5, 68, 70, 72, 74, 78
   coloured, 53, 62, 63–5, 74
burr, 30, 33–4, 35, 83

carving (*see also* fancy sticks), 7, 19, 21, 22–3, 30,
   31, 32, 86
checks, 9, 10, 14, 34, 80
cherry, 11
clamps, 19, 56, 57–9
collars, 29, 43, 47, 74, 77–8
cow horn, 28, 50–1, 63, 74, 77
crooks, 21, 24, 25, 26, 27, 28, 29, 30, 31, 33, 35, 48,
   49, 50, 56, 58, 59, 60, 61, 62, 67, 68, 73, 74, 88,
   89, 90
crown, 24, 26, 27, 28, 30, 56, 57, 58, 59, 60, 61, 62,
   64, 69, 73

deer antler, 29, 36–45, 63, 64, 77, 78, 79, 81, 83,
   86, 91, 92
dolly (cylinder), *55*, 57–60

dowel, 17, 28, 43, 44, 45, 75–7

elm, 30, 31, 33
emery, 20, 26, 65, 80

fancy sticks, 20, 31, 32, 66–72, 87–90, 91, 92
ferrule, 78–9, 90
finish, 80–1, 90
flat-bit drills, 17, 43, 75
foreign timbers, 31
formers, 19, 23, 24, 56, 58, 59, 60, 61,
   62, 63

galls, 34
glue, 26, 34, 43, 45, 46, 47, 51, 67, 68, 70, 74, 75,
   76, 77, 78, 79, 80, 91, 92
grain, 9, 10, 11, 12, 27, 30, 31, 33, 34

horn (*see also* billy-goat, buffalo and cow), 15, 17,
   18, 19, 28, 48–74, 77, 78, 79, 80, 81, 83, 84, 85,
   88, 89, 90, 91, 92
half head, 69–72
half stick, 27–8
hawthorn, 10–11, 31
hazel, 8–9, 12, 14, 21, 23, 24, 25, 31, 33
holly, 9–10, 11, 12, 14, 21, 23, 24, 25, 29, 31, 33,
   83, 92
honeysuckle twist, 22, 30
hot-air gun, 13, 18, 23, 25, 26, 36, 56, 73

joints, 28, 29, 43, 47, 73, 75–7, 90
judging, 87–90
juniper, 30, 31, 32

knives, 7, 14, 16, 17, 19, 76
knob sticks, 10, 21
knots, 10, 11, 12, 76, 80
knotting (knot sealer), 9, 25, 34

laburnum, 30
laurel, 30, 31
leg crook, 27, 61
length, 8, 10, 11
lime, 30

market stick, 25, 50, 56, 58, 61, 62
mountain ash (rowan), 11, 31

neck, 56, 57, 58, 59, 60, 61, 63, 64, 68, 69
nose, 27, 50, 56, 58, 59, 60, 61, 62, 64, *66*, 67, 68, 74, 92

oak, 13, 31, 33, 34

painting, 20, 31, 32, 69, 70, 72, 93
pear, 11
pyrography, 19, 68, 70, 72

ram's curl, 61–2, 63
ram's horn, 48–50, 52, 53, 54–62, 74, 88, 91
root, 21, 23

sash cramp, 19, 20, 54, 56, 59, *60*, 61, 62, 65
saws, 14, 16, 19
seasoning
    wood, 8, 9, 11–12, 14, 21, 25, 31, 34

horn, 49
shows, 7, 15, 87–90
spacers, 29, 43, 78, 92
spruce, 11
squeezing up, 50, 51, 52, 55–8
stains
    coffee, 9, 11, 12, 26, 31, 32, 44
    permanganate of potash, 12, 43, 44
steel wool, 9, 20, 80
storage, 12
straightening, 12–14
strapping, 20, 26, 80
studding, 28, 75

taper, 9, 10, 11
thumbsticks, 21, 30, 31, 35, 36, 38, 40, 41, 42
tools, 7, 14, 15–20
tufnol, 65

varnish, 81, 86, 90

walnut, 30, 31, 32
whistle stick handle, 44–5
workshop, 15, 20

yew, 11, 30, 32